THE

Quotable

SOUTHERNER

THE

Quotable

SOUTHERNER

Centuries of Wit and Wisdom

POLLY POWERS STRAMM

Globe
Pequot

Guilford, Connecticut

Globe
Pequot

An imprint of The Rowman & Littlefield Publishing Group, Inc.
4501 Forbes Blvd., Ste. 200
Lanham, MD 20706
www.rowman.com

Distributed by NATIONAL BOOK NETWORK

British Library Cataloguing in Publication Information available

Library of Congress Cataloging-in-Publication Data available

ISBN 978-1-4930-4539-6 (paperback)
ISBN 978-1-4930-4540-2 (e-book)

♾™ The paper used in this publication meets the minimum requirements of American National Standard for Information Sciences—Permanence of Paper for Printed Library Materials, ANSI/NISO Z39.48-1992.

CONTENTS

ACKNOWLEDGMENTS

When I casually mentioned to friends and colleagues that I was writing a book filled with Southerners' quotes, a good many of those buddies patted me on the back and gave me plenty of tight congratulatory hugs. Several offered advice, suggestions, and assistance because that's simply the way it is in the South. Friends, family, and even perfect strangers will go above and beyond to help their fellow man or woman.

I couldn't have put this book together without the kindness of pals who dropped off gifts such as wine, candles, and insanely delicious pralines to ensure that I had the proper atmosphere and relaxed temperament for researching and writing.

The idea of *The Quotable Southerner* came from Amy Lyons, my wonderful and enthusiastic editor at Globe Pequot, who approached me with this fabulous idea. She offered a few guidelines and turned me loose to compile what I consider a fun and interesting volume. I am a lucky gal to have such a talented editor.

It goes without saying that I must thank my dear family, who always is supportive and excited about every writing assignment I tackle. As luck would have it—or maybe not—while I was working on this book, our contractor friend decided he finally had the time and inclination to build a screened porch for us. (A screened porch in the South is a necessity if you want to relax outside in the spring and summer. Gnats and mosquitoes will carry you away without one.)

Meanwhile, another team of workers decided they were ready to both redo our kitchen and scrape the ugly textured design from our ceilings. I figured the addition and refurbishment wouldn't take long or inconvenience us, but, boy howdy, was I wrong. We basically had to pack up everything in our house until the renovation and construction jobs were finished. More than two months later and several layers of choking dust, our home improvement projects were completed. In fact, I wrote the last few chapters of this book on my new screened porch, enjoying the stir of a slight spring breeze while listening to birds singing in my backyard.

While the house was being transformed, I was too busy yelling at workers to be able to do much book work, but as the deadline approached, my husband, Steve, and our daughters, Polly and Mary, took over tying up loose ends so I could hunker down and write. When need be, there's nothing quite like supportive family and an understanding editor.

INTRODUCTION

Take it from me—figuring out what boundaries define the South and what makes a Southerner definitely aren't easy tasks. The US Census Bureau has come up with a list of sixteen states that it has declared to be the South: Delaware, Florida, Georgia, North Carolina, South Carolina, Maryland, Virginia, West Virginia, Alabama, Kentucky, Mississippi, Tennessee, Arkansas, Louisiana, Oklahoma, and Texas.

Meanwhile, historians are convinced that the South includes the eleven states (and one territory) that seceded before or during the Civil War and established the Confederate States of America (CSA). That list omits Maryland, Delaware, West Virginia, and Kentucky, with Oklahoma as the territory at the time.

Some folks may disagree with both the historians and the Census Bureau, but, as a Southern girl hailing from Georgia, the Census Bureau list suits me just fine. Or, as a wise old friend once old me, "It's close enough for government work." I do have one thing weighing on my mind, though. What about those people who were born elsewhere, say up north or out west, who moved to the South as infants, or vice versa? Are they adopted Southerners? What about the snowbirds from the North and Midwest who now call Florida home? I like to believe that some of those transplanted people could be just as Southern as the rest of us.

Think of former president George W. Bush, poet Carl Sandburg, or Larry the Cable Guy. Bush was born in Connecticut but grew up in Texas; Sandburg was born in Chicago but spent the last years of his life in North Carolina, where he did a whole bunch of writing; Larry the Cable Guy puts on a good act of being a good ole boy from the South, but he was actually born in Nebraska. As he explains: "I went to college in Georgia, so I picked up the Southern accent. I talked like that with my friends all the time, because it was fun. It was funny . . . All my friends were real Southern. We're buddies, so I'd say stuff to make them laugh. So that was pretty much it."

Who is a Southerner and who's not is a conundrum, for sure. I tend to think that being labeled a Southerner is a state of mind, and certainly so if you're not born in one of the states listed as being in the South. As singer-songwriter Darius Rucker says in the song (coincidentally entitled "Southern State of Mind"):

I could be anywhere.
In my heart I'm always there.
Where you know everybody and if
you don't you're still polite.
No changin' who I am, that's the way I've always been.
No matter what state I'm in,
I'm in a Southern state of mind.

Next there was the matter of selecting the quotes to go with the topics. I decided to mix in a sprinkling of serious statements with humorous comments, because every Southerner worth his or her weight in gold has a mighty fine sense of humor. I certainly learned a great deal about the people of the South (and those adopted Southerners) while doing research for this book. My hope is that you will find out more about this wonderful region of the country that I am fortunate to call home. Moreover, I hope both my words and the people I quote in these pages will have a profound effect on your emotions and you'll laugh, nod your head in agreement, or maybe wipe a tear from your cheek.

Whatever the region is called—Old South, New South, the Deep South, or (Lord have mercy) Dixie, among other nicknames, it's an area known for warm hospitality, a colorful history, a rich and varied landscape, rib-sticking food, a place with both an avid sports base and a devotion to religion, and patriotism. On the following pages, I'll share quotes on those topics and more, including civil rights and justice, relationships and family, as well as romance and love, and life and death.

I'll wrap it all up with a list of homegrown advice and descriptions of life in the South offered by natives and outsiders, like poet Walt Whitman of New York, who wrote this poem:

O magnet-South! O glistening
perfumed South! My South!
O quick mettle, rich blood, impulse and love!
Good and evil! O all dear to me . . .
A Kentucky corn-field, the tall, graceful,
long-leav'd corn, slender,
flapping, bright green, with tassels, with
beautiful ears each well-sheath'd in its husk;
O my heart! O tender and fierce pangs, I
can stand them not, I will depart;
O to be a Virginian where I grew
up! O to be a Carolinian!
O longings irrepressible! O I will go back to
old Tennessee and never wander more.

CHAPTER 1

The People of the South and Their Unique Character

If you ask a Southerner to describe one of their own, you best plan to sit a spell, because most folks from the South are natural-born storytellers. Add a delicious drawl that will stop you in your tracks, and—in a New York minute—you'll be mesmerized. That drawl is different even within the South. Someone from the Georgia coast has a different accent than someone from Charleston, South Carolina, and a Charlestonian sounds nothing like someone from the North Carolina mountains.

Wherever they're from and whatever their accent, Southerners love to talk to anyone and everyone. They're both honest and kind to a fault, and are known to speak their minds and take their time with nary an apology. To a Southerner, good manners are a must. In a blog for the *Houston Chronicle*, Marcy De Luna listed "Things We Do in the South that Northerners Just Don't Get": "The gentlemanly arts include opening doors and car doors for women (just because we can do it ourselves doesn't mean we want to), offering us a chair, and walking on the outside of a sidewalk so we're safe from traffic."

Even without a proper introduction, a Southerner might strike up a conversation and start telling you—in glorious detail—how they think, what they know, and whatever it is they're planning to do. When they dish out their opinions—accessorized with a grand gift of gab—they don't hold back for anything. They're loud and proud of their heritage, faith, and families. People in other parts of the country might snicker and call this quality an affliction, but down South, we refer to their jabbering as attitude, advice, or plain ole sass.

Visualize a gathering of men chewing the fat in a barbershop or a gaggle of women having their hair washed and set at the neighborhood beauty parlor. Or, picture a few guys playing checkers while sitting on overturned buckets under a couple of pecan trees. Chances are, all those men and women are chatting about this 'n' that and coming up with descriptions of their Southern style that could fill volumes.

Charles Kuralt of CBS News hit it right on the mark in *Southerners: Portrait of a People*: "In the South, the breeze blows softer ... neighbors are friendlier, and more talkative. (By contrast with the Yankee, the Southerner never uses one word when ten or twenty will do) ... This is a different place. Our way of thinking is different, as are our ways of seeing, laughing, singing, eating, meeting and parting. Our walk is different, as the old song goes, our talk and our names."

* * *

Southerners love a good tale. They are born reciters, great memory retainers, diary keepers, letter exchangers . . . great talkers.

—Eudora Welty, writer

Because I was born in the South, I'm a Southerner. If I had been born in the North, the West or the Central Plains, I would just be a human being.

—Clyde Edgerton, writer

I love being Southern because of the people and the fans we have. People down here are more friendly—really warm people.

—Gary Rossington, founder of the Southern rock band, Lynyrd Skynyrd

The only place in the world that nothing has to be explained to me is the South.

—Woodrow Wilson, twenty-sixth president of the United States

This "Whoa, Nellie!" thing is overrated. There were all kinds of stories going around. People said I had a mule in Georgia named Nellie. Well, we had a mule in Georgia, but her name was Pearl.

—Keith Jackson, sportscaster

And what we students of history always learn is that the human being is a very complicated contraption and that they are not good or bad but are good and bad and the good comes out of the bad and the bad out of the good, and the devil take the hindmost.

—Robert Penn Warren, *All the King's Men*

Southern girls are God's gift to the entire male population. There is absolutely no woman finer than one raised below the Mason–Dixon line, and once you go Southern, may the good Lord help you never go back.

–Kenny Chesney, singer

Being Southern isn't talking with an accent . . . or rocking on a porch while drinking sweet tea, or knowing how to tell a good story. It's how you're brought up–with Southerners, family (blood kin or not) is sacred; you respect others and are polite nearly to a fault; you always know your place but are fierce about your beliefs. And food–along with college football–is darn near a religion.

–Jan Norris, writer

These were people who remembered the weight of the cotton sack, people with grease under their fingernails that no amount of Octagon soap would ever scrub away, people who built redwood decks on their mobile homes and have no idea that smart-aleck Yankees think that is somehow funny. People of the pines. My people.

–Rick Bragg, author, *All Over But the Shoutin'*

We Southerners live at a leisurely pace and sharing our hospitality with our family, friends, and the stranger within our gate is one of our greatest joys.

—Winifred G. Cheney, writer

There are so many colorful characters in Florida. There's a lot of money, development—not all of it good—and corruption.

—John Grisham, writer

Some people take me as being a rowdy, honky-tonk hero type. Some people see me as a quiet person. I guess I can be either one, you know, at any moment.

—Dickey Betts, former member of
The Allman Brothers Band

In New Orleans I have noticed that people are happiest when they are going to funerals, making money, taking care of the dead, or putting on masks at Mardi Gras so nobody knows who they are.

—Walker Percy, author, *Lancelot*

Shoot, man, I loved being a damn heel. Something about that, just going out there and being the most despicable person you could ever be, was a real turn-on for me. And I grew up a real shy kid in south Texas, and it was something for me to lean on and have fun with.

—"Stone Cold" Steve Austin, former professional wrestler

Never let it be said that dialect is a reflection of intellect. On the contrary, it is a reflection of the deep traditional values of a culture that respects family, God, and a language system above everything else. I give thanks to my maker that I'm a Southern woman.

—Patricia H. Graham, writer

I was born in Dallas, Texas, but I was raised in south Florida. "Ice Ice Baby" is about that area.

—Vanilla Ice, musician

I learned a long time ago that you don't have to go around using bad language and trying to hurt people to show how macho you are. That stuff won't get you anywhere; it just shows lack of vocabulary and character.

—Bobby Bowden, former football coach,
Florida State University

My mother's people, the people who captured my imagination when I was growing up, were of the Deep South—emotional, changeable, touched with charisma and given to histrionic flourishes. They were courageous under tension and unexpectedly tough beneath their wild eccentricities, for they had an unusually close working agreement with God. They also had an unusually high quota of bullshit.

—Willie Morris, author

On Christmas morning, before we could open our Christmas presents, we would go to this stranger's home and bring them presents. I remember helping clean the house up and putting up a tree. My father believed that you have a responsibility to look after everyone else.

—George Clooney, actor

It took me a long time to realize these people were genuine, true characters. I'd bring home friends and their jaws would drop. *Oh my gosh, your aunt, your uncle.* And I was like, *What?* I didn't realize there was anything different about them. I couldn't see it. Once I went out into the wider world, I was like, *Yeah, I guess they are kind of interesting people.*

—Tig Notaro, *Garden & Gun*

I'm a country boy. I'm from Georgia.

—Jason Aldean, singer

Despite the sarcastic remarks of Northerners, who don't know the region (read Easterners, Westerners, North Easterners, North Westerners, Midwesterners), the South of the United States can be so impellingly beautiful that sophisticated creature comforts diminish in importance.

—Maya Angelou, author, *Gather Together in My Name*

I always told people Alabama was the smartest state because it has four As and a B.

—Dabo Swinney, football coach at Clemson University

Great things happen in small places. Jesus was born in Bethlehem. Jesse Jackson was born in Greenville.

—Jesse Jackson, activist

Yes, sir. I'm a real Southern boy. I got a red neck, white socks, and Blue Ribbon beer.

—Billy Carter, brother of Jimmy Carter, thirty-ninth president of the United States

I'd sooner wear white shoes in February, drink unsweetened tea, and eat Miracle Whip instead of Duke's than utter the word "you guys."

—Celia Rivenbark, author, *Bless Your Heart, Tramp: And Other Southern Endearments*

Always marry a woman from Texas. No matter how tough things get, she's seen tougher.

—Dan Rather, journalist

She was so Southern that she cried tears that came straight from the Mississippi and she always smelled faintly of cottonwood and peaches.

—Sarah Addison Allen, author, *Garden Spells*

Oh, all Southern women say they're sorry. You could do almost anything—bump into someone, don't spread the jam right—you're always sorry. I've had people tell me to stop saying it so much.

—Andie MacDowell, actress

I was the fattest baby in Clark County, Arkansas. They put me in the newspaper. It was like a prize turnip.

—Billy Bob Thornton, actor and director

There's a Southern accent, where I come from
The young 'uns call it country, the Yankees call it dumb.
I got my own way of talking, but everything gets done
With a Southern accent, where I come from.

—Tom Petty, musician, "Southern Accents"

My career still strikes me as miraculous. That a boy raised on Marine bases in the South, taught by Roman Catholic nuns in backwater Southern towns that loathed Catholics, and completed his education with an immersion into The Citadel—the whole story sounds fabricated, impossible even to me. Maybe especially to me.

—Pat Conroy, author,
A Lowcountry Heart: Reflections on a Writing Life

Everyone in the South has no time for reading because they are all too busy writing.

—William Faulkner, writer

Deep down, I'm a Texas girl looking for that big romance every girl dreams about. Biologically, I look forward to being a cornerstone of a family. I'll be in my glory when I have a child on my knee.

—Renee Zellweger, actress

Southern people are raised with a work ethic. My son is five years old and does chores. My mom was a dance teacher, and the training and discipline it takes to be a dancer I've carried with me in Hollywood.

—Jaime Pressly, actress

Fincher was the kind of Southerner who will try to address you through a web of deep and antic Southernness, and who assumes everybody in earshot knows all about his parents and history and wants to hear an update about them at every opportunity. He looks young, but still manages to act sixty-five.

—Richard Ford, author, *The Sportswriter*

I'm not a person who naturally loves to wake up in the morning and go "Yeah, I'm going to work out for five hours—wooh!" Like, that's not my thing. I'm from Texas. I like to eat carbs. I like to chill out with my friends and do anything but 150 push-ups and sit-ups.

—Jennifer Love Hewitt, actress

I don't think a man has to go around shouting and playacting to prove he is something. And a real man don't go around putting other guys down, trampling their feelings in the dirt, making out they're nothing.

—Joe Frazier, former professional boxer

The first trip I can remember would have to be to Marianna, Arkansas. My mother's parents are from there, and we'd go every year to visit the church where they were buried. We'd attend church service that day, put flowers around their tombstones, and visit with family and friends that still lived there.

—Sterling K. Brown, actor

To be born a Southern woman is to be made aware of your distinctiveness. And with it, the rules. The expectations. These vary some, but all follow the same template, which is, fundamentally, no matter what the circumstance, Southern women make the effort. Which is why even the girls in the trailer parks paint their nails. And why overstressed working moms still bake three dozen homemade cookies for the school fund-raiser. And why you will never see Reese Witherspoon wearing sweatpants. Or Oprah take a nap.

—Allison Glock, author

I am proud of being a Southerner. I wasn't about to let Southerners on my show be stupid or aw-shuckses who just sit on the front porch and spit in the yard. I wasn't about to do that, and I made that very clear from the start. I was kind of the gatekeeper on that stuff.

—Andy Griffith, actor

'Cause a Mississippi girl don't change her ways
Just 'cause everybody knows her name
Ain't bigheaded from a little bit of fame
I still like wearing my old ball cap
Riding my kids around piggyback
They might know me all around the world
But, y'all, I'm still a Mississippi girl.

—Faith Hill, singer, "Mississippi Girl"

I'm still the little Southern girl from the wrong side of the tracks who really didn't feel like she belonged.

—Faye Dunaway, actress

I think everybody wants to be proud of where they're from. I remember having to deal with this when I moved up North. When you move to New York City with an accent like mine, people think you're kinda dumb. After they figured out I could put a complex sentence together, then I was fine and they were curious about me. My accent became a little more charming, I suppose.

—Chuck Reece, "The Bitter Southerner"

A ship is always referred to as "she" because it costs so much to keep one in paint and powder.

—Navy admiral Chester W. Nimitz

Growing up in Georgia, I used to think people up north or out west were so different. They're really not. They're just regular people who live in small towns. They grow up and try to raise families and have a job and go to church and play softball. It's that way everywhere.

—Alan Jackson, singer

Although no one believes me, I have always been a country girl and still have a country girl's values.

—Ava Gardner, actress

The tradition of the South is not urban . . . I think we are a region of storytellers, naturally, just from our tribal instincts. We did not have the pleasures of the theater or the dance, motion pictures when they came along. We simply entertain each other by talking.

—Harper Lee, author

Right is right, even if no one else does it.
—Juliette Gordon Low,
founder of the Girl Scouts

I like the South: Southern literature and that relationship between grotesqueness and living below the Mason–Dixon line. But I also understand that people view it as a limitation—as an actor and as a person—perceptions that are really wrong: that you are ignorant and possibly illiterate, or that it's cute.

—Holly Hunter, actress

To identify a person as a Southerner suggests not only that her history is inescapable and formative, but that it is also impossibly present. Southerners live uneasily at the nexus between myth and reality, watching the mishmash amalgam of sorrow, humility, honor, graciousness, and renegade defiance play out against a backdrop of profligate physical beauty.

—Sally Mann, author, *Deep South*

Smokey and the Bandit was just a lark. All we did was run up and down those Georgia roads wrecking cars and having the time of our life.

—Jerry Reed, singer and actor

With the accent, it's an internal dialogue that Southerners have with themselves. We kind of carry around that shame, that feeling of being inferior to the North. I think I did lose some of the accent for a while. Because when I was a graduate student, I was terrified at having to get up in front of a roomful of smart New York kids.

—Bobbie Ann Mason, author

Living in a small Italian hilltown, and having lived in a small town in south Georgia, I understand that you can recognize a family gene pool by the lift of an eyebrow, or the length of a neck, or a way of walking.

—Frances Mayes, author

My characters aren't grotesque. That's just the way people are in the South.
—Flannery O'Connor, author

South Carolina is too small for a republic and too large for an insane asylum.

—James L. Petigru, former attorney general of South Carolina

Texas is OK if you want to settle down and do your own thing quietly, but it's not for outrageous people, and I was always outrageous.

–Janis Joplin, singer

I think we Southerners have talked a fair amount of malarkey about the mystique of being Southern.

–Reynolds Price, poet

Growing up with country, R&B, gospel, and classical music from my grandmother and pop, Tuskegee was the perfect melting pot for my influences as a writer.

–Lionel Richie, musician

I grew up partially around Stone Mountain, Georgia, and in that part of the country, there was always this aura of mythology and palpable sense of otherness about being a Southerner.

–Kara Walker, artist

My father was a gambler down in Georgia,
And he wound up on the wrong end of a gun,
And I was born in the backseat of a Greyhound bus,
Rollin' down Highway 41.
–Dickey Betts of The Allman Brothers Band,
"Ramblin' Man"

I grew up in a small town in coastal South Carolina. Where I'm from, the people are known as Gullah people. They're some of the first freed slaves that lived on their own, without being attached to the rest of the US.

—Brian Stelfreeze, artist

Even today, the South is quirky, quick to take offense, fanciful: it has an attitude, a frame of mind. It prefers the flowery to the plain, likes its own jokes, its own rhetoric. It can laugh at itself at home, but it is immediately riled at any snicker from outside.

—Eugene Walter, author

What I am writing about is human nature. I write about the South because I think the war between romanticism and the hostility to it is very sharp there.

—Tennessee Williams, writer

Tough girls come from New York. Sweet girls, they're from Georgia. But us Kentucky girls, we have fire and ice in our blood. We can ride horses, be a debutante, throw left hooks, and drink with the boys, all the while making sweet tea, darlin'. And if we have an opinion, you know you're gonna hear it.

—Ashley Judd, actress

From the mountains of Virginia to the Texas Plains there is a Southern way of life, and it begins with hospitality and a proper emphasis on good cooking.

—Winifred G. Cheney, writer

Being a Southern person and a blonde, it's not a good combination. Immediately, when people meet you, they think of you as not being smart.

—Reese Witherspoon, actress

As a child in South Carolina, I spent summers like so many children—sitting on my grandparents' back porch with my siblings, spitting watermelon seeds into the garden or, even worse, swallowing them and trembling as my older brother and sister spoke of the vine that was probably already growing in my belly.

—Jacqueline Woodson, writer

CHAPTER 2

History and Such

To say the South has a complicated history is a humongous understatement. Of course, the history of the South can't ever be discussed without addressing what has become the giant elephant in the room: the Civil War.

The war, or whatever it may be referred to as—the War Between the States, the War of Northern Aggression, the War to Preserve the Union, or the War of Southern Rebellion, to name a few—always seems to be that pachyderm in perpetual pain that nobody—or everybody—wants to talk about. If Southerners do want to debate the war, you can count on raised voices and clenched fists and some mumbling that the South shall rise again.

Even more than one hundred years later, a dialogue about the Civil War conjures up a wide range of emotions and feelings—hate, anger, sadness, disgust, happiness, and pride—for Southerners as well as those who live in other regions of the United States and tend to want to judge the South.

Long before 1861, when Fort Sumter was fired upon in Charleston harbor and the Civil War began, Southerners were chronicling bits and pieces of history.

When colonies and territories were discovered and when they joined the Union are two different entities. For that reason, Southern states boast a hodgepodge of early residents—Native Americans, Mexicans, and European explorers.

The state of Georgia, for example, was founded in 1733 by Englishman James E. Oglethorpe, who set foot in Savannah where he was greeted by Yamacraw Indian chief Tomochichi and his interpreter, Mary Musgrove. More than sixty years prior to Oglethorpe's arrival, in what is now the Carolinas, eight English nobles settled the region to claim it for King Charles II. All of those areas didn't join the Union until much later.

Prior to Oglethorpe befriending Tomochichi—in 1565, to be exact—Spanish explorers stumbled upon a place they christened St. Augustine, Florida. Not to be outdone, the English arrived in Jamestown, Virginia, in 1607, making that settlement the first English one in the New World. A little more than ten years later, the first Africans came by ship to Virginia. Meanwhile, things began cooking out west in 1718 when the Alamo and San Antonio, Texas, were established.

The 1700s also saw the formation of the Mason–Dixon line, which divides the North from the South. Tennessee and Kentucky were developed, and the Continental Army—consisting of Virginia, the Carolinas, and Georgia—was established. The South played many roles in the American Revolution, including the Siege of Savannah and the Battle of Cowpens.

The Civil War began because of political and cultural differences, such as slavery, and was a series of bloody battles that lasted from 1861 to 1865. In the South, Rebel and Union soldiers fought at places with colorful names like Chickamauga and Appomattox Courthouse. The burning of Atlanta occurred when Union general William Tecumseh Sherman made his famous March through Georgia, igniting everything in his way, except for Savannah, which he presented to President Abraham Lincoln as a Christmas gift.

After the war, Reconstruction began, and the South struggled to get back on its feet. The twentieth century brought the Great Depression of the 1930s, and civil rights advancements beginning in the 1950s, with the US Supreme Court decision in *Brown v. Board of Education*. Additionally, more rural areas became industrialized, a trend that continues today.

* * *

The preservation of the sacred fire of liberty, and the destiny of the Republican model of Government, are justly considered as deeply, perhaps as finally staked, on the experiment entrusted to the hands of the American people.

—George Washington, first president of the United States

Is life so dear or peace so sweet as to be purchased at the price of chains and slavery? Forbid it, Almighty God! I know not what course others may take, but as for me, give me liberty, or give me death!

—Patrick Henry, politician

The planter, the farmer, the mechanic, and the laborer . . . form the great body of the people of the United States, they are the bone and sinew of the country men who love liberty and desire nothing but equal rights and equal laws.

> —Andrew Jackson, seventh president of the United States

He is a scoundrel and a lying rascal.

> —General Lachlan McIntosh's assessment of Button Gwinnett, whom he shot in a duel (Gwinnett was a Signer of the Declaration of Independence from Georgia and interim governor of the colony when he died)

Quite often, people inaccurately comment about the villains of the South and the heroes of the North. Such statements cause bitter debates. Thus, it is important to recognize the good and the bad from both the Confederate and Union armies. The fact is, the war stripped many men of their inhibitions and their immoral behaviors detrimentally affected all fellow Americans.

> —Trevor P. Wardlaw, author,
> *Sires and Sons: The Story of Hubbard's Regiment*

It is of great importance to our country generally, and especially to our navigating and whaling interests, that the Pacific Coast and, indeed, the whole of our territory west of the Rocky Mountains, should speedily be filled up by a hardy and patriotic population.

> —James K. Polk, eleventh president of the United States

My great-grandfather and his two brothers fought at Gettysburg. They were in artillery, and they survived the war, thank goodness. So I revere what they did. I think their motivations were honorable when they undertook the war and participated in it along with other Southerners.

—Jimmy Carter, thirty-ninth president of the United States

Nothing fills me with deeper sadness than to see a Southerner apologizing for the defense we made of our inheritance.

—Jefferson Davis, president of the
Confederate States of America

As a Southerner I would have to say that one of the main importances of the War is that Southerners have a sense of defeat which none of the rest of the country has.
—Shelby Foote, writer

In the South, history clings to you like a wet blanket. Outside your door the past awaits in Indian mounds, plantation ruins, heaving sidewalks and homestead graveyards; each slowly reclaimed by the kudzu of time.

—Tim Heaton, author, *Don't Be Ugly*

In the Confederate Army, an officer was judged by
stark courage alone, and this made it possible for the
Confederacy to live four years.
            —US Marine Corps lieutenant general Chesty Puller

The care of human life and happiness, and not their
destruction, is the first and only object of good government.
      —Thomas Jefferson, third president of the United States

A Union that can only be maintained by
swords and bayonets, and in which strife and
civil war are to take the place of brotherly
love and kindness, has no charm for me.
          —Gen. Robert E. Lee, commander
              of the Confederate States Army

Our country may be likened to a new house. We lack many
things, but we possess the most precious of all—liberty.
            —James Monroe, fifth president of the United States

My arm extended upward in pleading for peace and the
Union of our Fathers . . . When my hand came down from
that impassioned gesticulation, it fell slowly and sadly by the
side of a Secessionist.
                  —Zebulon Vance Baird, Civil War soldier
                      and governor of North Carolina

Without the firing of a gun, without drawing a sword, should they [Northerners] make war upon us [Southerners], we could bring the whole world to our feet. What would happen if no cotton was furnished for three years? . . . England would topple headlong and carry the whole civilized world with her. No, you dare not make war on cotton! No power on earth dares make war upon it. Cotton is King.

–James Henry Hammond,
US senator from South Carolina, in an 1858 letter to
Senator William H. Seward of New York

Every man should endeavor to understand the meaning of subjugation before it is too late . . . It means the history of this heroic struggle will be written by the enemy; that our youth will be trained by Northern schoolteachers; will learn from Northern school books their version of the war; will be impressed by the influences of history and education to regard our gallant dead as traitors, and our maimed veterans as fit objects for derision . . . It is said slavery is all we are fighting for, and if we give it up we give up all. Even if this were true, which we deny, slavery is not all our enemies are fighting for. It is merely the pretense to establish sectional superiority and a more centralized form of government, and to deprive us of our rights and liberties.

–Maj. Gen. Patrick R. Cleburne, CSA, January 1864

When a nation has just emerged from the
throes of a great civil warfare, where section
was arrayed against section, class against class,
two things are to be done: First, the work of
reconstruction is to be effected; secondly,
a willingness for the proper acceptance of
the issue's decision is to be created.
—Lucius Quintus Cincinnatus Lamar II, soldier,
politician, and former US Supreme Court justice

No matter what rallying cries the orators give to the idiots
who fight, no matter what noble purposes they assign to
wars, there is never but one reason for a war. And that is
money.

—Margaret Mitchell, author, *Gone with the Wind*

He fought the fight to finish,
And his soldier's work is done;
Lee ever stands immortal!
Freedom's model of a son.
As in the day of battle,
Or on his great retreat,
The center of attraction;
We come, our Lee to meet.
—R. H. Dykers, "Lee"

Soldiers, I intend to stay here, not only as long as a man remains, but as long as a piece of a man is left.
—Zachary Taylor, twelfth president of the United States

Under the ominous shadow which the Second World War and its attendant circumstances have cast on the world, peace has become as essential to civilized existence as the air we breathe is to life itself.
—Cordell Hull, former US secretary of
state under Franklin D. Roosevelt

CHAPTER 3

Landscape and Weather

The Southern United States is blessed to have a long list of gorgeous natural resources, including statuesque mountains, rolling hills, pristine streams, tumbling rivers, and green pastures. The haunting swamps of Georgia and Florida, the mysterious bayous of Louisiana, and the beaches of the Atlantic Ocean and Gulf of Mexico help shape the Southern landscape.

The South is home to the Great Smoky Mountains located along the Tennessee and North Carolina border. With more than eleven million visitors a year, the Great Smoky Mountains National Park is the most visited national park in the United States. The range has been immortalized in song and poetry, just as have the Shenandoah Mountains in Virginia and West Virginia.

The South also has some pretty unique geographical features, like the Okefenokee Swamp in Georgia and Florida, which is the largest blackwater swamp in North America. Florida's Everglades is the largest tropical wilderness in the country. In her book, *The Everglades: River of Grass*, Marjory Stoneman Douglas describes the area: "The miracle of light pours over the green and brown expanse of saw grass and of water, shining and slowly moving, the grass and water that is the meaning and the central fact of the Everglades. It is a river of grass."

Fields of crops, such as cotton, corn, tobacco, peanuts, and soybeans, provide an even more picturesque backdrop for the region. Those who grow up in the

South recall summertime as meaning hours in the family car bouncing along blacktop roads with green fields on either side extending for miles.

In an interview in *Garden & Gun* magazine, businesswoman and philanthropist Darla Moore recalled part of her youth: "I spent most of my time with my grandparents on their farm. Tobacco was the great cash crop and produced what prosperity there was for a long, long time. I loved it—being on a working farm. The activity of it. My poor grandmother's good silver. I would take spoons out and dig mud holes. It was the happiest place of my life—the most comforting, peaceful place."

The region also has a few head-turning attractions, such as the life-size bronze statue of Dolly Parton in front of the county courthouse in Sevierville, Tennessee. Over in Georgia a statue of Br'er Rabbit stands on the courthouse lawn in Eatonton.

In Gatlinburg, Tennessee, there's Cooter's Place, which is sort of a store/museum that shows off memorabilia from *The Dukes of Hazzard* TV show. Down in Florida, the list of theme parks and attractions is practically endless, with Walt Disney World leading the pack. Others include Universal Studios, Sea World, Busch Gardens, and Legoland.

For the most part, the weather in the South is mild year-round, but summers and early fall can be hot as Hades and bring the fury of killer hurricanes to the Atlantic or Gulf coasts. In the winter it's not unusual for snow to fall in the states that lie closest to the Mason–Dixon line. When a freakish snowstorm hits places like Birmingham, Alabama, or Charleston, South Carolina, residents don't know what to think or how to handle it, much less drive a vehicle on a road that has never seen a lick of salt.

* * *

Here in Florida the seasons move in and out like nuns in soft clothing, making no rustle in their passing.
  —Marjorie Kinnan Rawlings, author, *Cross Creek*

I have always had a love for American geography, and especially for the landscapes of the South. One of my pleasures has been to drive across it, with no one in the world knowing where I am, languidly absorbing the thoughts and memories of old moments, of people vanished now from my life.
  —Willie Morris, author, *The Courting of Marcus Dupree*

Growing up in Georgia, my dad was a farmer and we worked in agriculture, so we were always looking up at the sky, checking if rain was in the forecast. That always set the tone for the mood in my household, whether we had rain coming in or not—we knew the crops would be good and it was going to be a good week around the Bryan household.
  —Luke Bryan, musician

Southern nights
Have you ever felt a Southern night?
Free as a breeze
Not to mention the trees
Whistling tunes that you know and love so.
—Glen Campbell, "Southern Nights"

You know, in my hometown of Hope, Arkansas, the three sacred heroes were Jesus, Elvis, and FDR, not necessarily in that order.
—Mike Huckabee, former governor of Arkansas

Charlottesville is a quiet town with friendly people, good schools, lots of churches, parks, and a bustling, growing community that more or less revolves around one of the country's great public universities. Volunteerism is rampant, and dozens of nonprofits hustle about, solving problems and helping those in need.
—John Grisham, writer

It may sound funny, but I love the South. I don't choose to live anywhere else. There's land here, where a man can raise cattle, and I'm going to do it someday. There are lakes where a man can sink a hook and fight the bass. There is room here for my children to play and grow, and become good citizens—if the white man will let them.
—Medgar Evers, activist

My high school job was putting insulation in attics—in Louisiana in the summer. It must have been 95 degrees every day, and the insulation used to get all over me. It was not fun. But I didn't know any different. It wasn't like I was spending summers on Cape Cod.

—James Carville, political commentator
and media personality

I was born in a hurricane in Pensacola, Florida . . . my dad was in the military, so we moved all over the place. But I consider myself a Southerner from Louisiana. I've lived in Texas for most of my adult life.

—Kimberly Willis Holt, writer

We just kind of created our own thing and that's part of the beauty of Athens: is that it's so off the map and there's no way you could ever be the East Village or an L.A. scene or a San Francisco scene, that it just became its own thing.

—Michael Stipe, of the band R.E.M.

In my mind I'm gone to Carolina
Can't you see the sunshine?
Can't you just feel the moonshine?
Ain't it just like a friend of mine
To hit me from behind?
Yes, I'm gone to Carolina in my mind.

—James Taylor, "Carolina in My Mind"

It began to drizzle rain and he turned on the windshield wipers; they made a great clatter like two idiots clapping in church.

—Flannery O'Connor, author, *Wise Blood*

I grew up in Mobile, Alabama—somebody's got to be from Mobile, right?—and Mobile sits at the confluence of five rivers, forming this beautiful delta. And the delta has alligators crawling in and out of rivers filled with fish and cypress trees dripping with snakes, birds of every flavor.

—Mike DeGruy, American documentary filmmaker

The people of the State of Texas consist principally of men, women, and children, with a sprinkling of cowboys. The weather is very good, thermometer rarely rising above 2,500 degrees in the shade and hardly ever below 212.

—O. Henry, writer

I loved being outside. We'd hold lightning bugs in our fingers and pretend they were diamond rings.

—Loretta Lynn, singer

I have a sixty-acre farm in North Carolina, and I have a tractor and a farmhouse. As soon as I groom the land, I want to put cabins around and have a place where people can write and hang out. It'll be either that or an all-black nudist colony.

—Zach Galifianakis, actor

Smooth as the hickory wind
That blows from Memphis
Down to Apalachicola
It's hi y'all, did ya eat well
Come on in, I'm sure glad to know ya
Don't let this old gold cross
An' this Allman Brothers T-shirt throw ya
It's cicadas making noise
With the Southern voice.

—Tim McGraw, "Southern Voice"

A Southern moon is a sodden moon, and sultry. When it swamps the fields and the rustling sandy roads and the sticky honeysuckle hedges in its sweet stagnation, your fight to hold on to reality is like a protestation against a first waft of ether.

—Zelda Fitzgerald, *Save Me the Waltz*

My first job was cleaning dog kennels. It was especially, ah, aromatic during those hot, humid Louisiana summers, but it prepared me for Hollywood.

–Robert Crais, actor

I've been all over the world. I love New York, I love Paris, San Francisco, so many places. But there's no place like New Orleans. It's got the best food. It's got the best music. It's got the best people. It's got the most fun stuff to do.

–Harry Connick Jr., singer

We have to suffer mosquitoes the size of blackbirds.

–Rebecca Wells, writer

The Florida in my novels is not as seedy as the real Florida. It's hard to stay ahead of the curve. Every time I write a scene that I think is the sickest thing I have ever dreamed up, it is surpassed by something that happens in real life.

–Carl Hiaasen, writer

And Mama hollered out the back door,
Y'all, remember to wipe your feet
And then she said, I got some news this
mornin' from Choctaw Ridge
Today, Billy Joe MacAllister jumped
off the Tallahatchie Bridge.

–Bobbie Gentry, "Ode to Billie Joe"

I love Memphis, I guess you could say, in the way
that you love a brother even if he does sometimes
puzzle and sadden and frustrate you. Say what
you want about it, it's an authentic place. I was
born and raised in Memphis, and no matter
where I go, Memphis belongs to me, and I to it.
—Hampton Sides, writer

Moon River, wider than a mile
I'm crossing you in style, some day
Oh, dream maker, you heart breaker
Wherever you're goin', I'm goin' your way.
—Johnny Mercer, lyricist, "Moon River"

It's always on everyone's list, like, "What's New Orleans
like?" I think people have a preconceived idea, like it's just
Mardi Gras and Bourbon Street. But really, there's so much
culture, the music's great, the food's great. It's not good
for the waistline! But I'm actually from the South, I'm from
Georgia, so the weather doesn't bother me.
—Sung Kang, actor

I loved Mississippi and do to this day. The rainbows that
stretch from horizon to horizon after a summer rain are the
most spectacular I have ever seen.
—Charley Pride, author, *Pride: The Charley Pride Story*

Summer in the Deep South is not only a
season, a climate, it's a dimension. Floating in
it, one must be either proud or submerged.
—Eugene Walter, author, *The Untidy Pilgrim*

Sprinting for a full day in Atlanta in midsummer proved very
challenging. That humidity is crazy. Georgia is a beautiful
state, but the weather is intense. I was warned, but for some
reason I thought it would be like L.A. in the summer. The
reality? No.

—Theo James, actor

The sun shines bright in the old Kentucky home,
'Tis summer, the people are gay;
The corn-top's ripe and the meadow's in the bloom.
—Stephen Foster, "My Old Kentucky Home"

Maycomb was a tired old town, even in 1932 when I first
knew it. Somehow, it was hotter then. Men's stiff collars
wilted by nine in the morning. Ladies bathed before noon,
after their three o'clock naps, and by nightfall were like
soft teacakes with frosting from sweating and sweet talcum.
The day was twenty-four hours long, but it seemed longer.
There's no hurry, for there's nowhere to go and nothing to
buy . . . and no money to buy it with.

—Harper Lee, author, *To Kill a Mockingbird*

All my ex's live in Texas,
And Texas is the place I'd dearly love to be,
But all my ex's live in Texas,
Therefore I reside in Tennessee.
  —George Strait, "All My Ex's Live in Texas"

Growing up in Fitzgerald, I lived in an intense microcosm, where your neighbor knows what you're going to do even before you do, where you can recognize a family gene pool by the lift of an eyebrow, or the length of a neck, or a way of walking. What is said, what is left to the imagination, what is denied, withheld, exaggerated—all these secretive, inverted things informed my childhood. Writing the stories that I found in the box, I remember being particularly fascinated by secrets kept in order to protect someone from who you are. That protection, sharpest knife in the drawer, I absorbed as naturally as a Southern accent. At that time, I was curious to hold up to the light glimpses of the family that I had so efficiently fled. We were remote—back behind nowhere—when I was growing up, but even so, enormous social change was about to crumble foundations. Who were we, way far South? "We're south of everywhere," my mother used to lament.

  —Frances Mayes, author

There was a land of cavaliers and cotton fields called the Old South. Here in this pretty world, gallantry took its last bow. Here was the last ever to be seen of knights and their ladies fair, of master and of slave. Look for it only in books, for it is no more than a dream remembered, a civilization gone with the wind.

—Margaret Mitchell, prologue, *Gone with the Wind*

Down in the boondocks
Down in the boondocks
People put me down 'cause
That's the side of town I was born in.
I love her, she loves me, but I don't fit in her society
Lord have mercy on the boy from down in the boondocks.

—Billy Joe Royal, "Down in the Boondocks"

Nobody but a Southerner knows the wrenching rinsing sadness of the cities of the North.

—Walker Percy, author, *The Moviegoer*

I wonder if, north of here, they might even run out of stories someday. It may seem silly, but it is cold up there, too cold to mosey, to piddle, to loafer, and summer only lasts a week and a half. The people spit the words out so fast when they talk, like they are trying to discard them somehow, banish them, rather than relish the sound and the story. We will not run out of them here. We talk like we are tasting something.

–Rick Bragg, author, *My Southern Journey: True Stories from the Heart of the South*

Half of my family has a deep-rooted connection to the South and Louisiana, and for me, New Orleans is one of our most precious, historic communities: visually, emotionally, artistically.

–Sandra Bullock, actress

My parents live out in the middle of nowhere, in the middle of this peach orchard. It's actually Peach County, one of the largest peach-growing counties in Georgia. It's very rural, and there is nothing much going on, so I guess that's had a big influence on everything as far as just not having much to do.
–Washed Out, singer

Many Southern writers must have learned the art of storytelling from listening to oral tales. I did. It gave me the knowledge that the simplest incident can make a story.

—Erskine Caldwell, writer

Louisiana in September was like an obscene phone call from nature. The air—moist, sultry, secretive, and far from fresh—felt as if it were being exhaled into one's face. Sometimes it even sounded like heavy breathing.

—Tom Robbins, author, *Jitterbug Perfume*

Unfortunately, if you've ever been in southern Georgia on the beaches in a lightning storm, if you're out there, you're in great, great danger, and you can be killed very, very quickly.

—US Army general Norman Schwarzkopf

I said Georgia
Georgia
A song of you
Comes as sweet and clear
As moonlight through the pines . . .
    —Ray Charles, "Georgia on My Mind"

Annie Clyde had seen more than one tree uprooted in all this foul weather. She had heard the rain every way that it fell, hard like drumming fingers, in sheets like a long sigh, in spates like pebbles tossed at the windows. When she crossed the road and went up the bank, she could see water glinting between the tree stumps. The river had already become a lake.

    —Amy Greene, author, *Long Man*

CHAPTER 4

Food That Will Have You Beggin' for Seconds

Fried chicken, cornbread, black-eyed peas, and home-made biscuits are as Southern as all get out, and in recent years those kinds of rib-sticking dishes have spread to places throughout the United States.

In short, Southern cuisine is cool.

Restaurants and diners specializing in mouthwatering Southern fare are popping up left and right throughout the country. In New York City, for example, a fellow born and reared in Alabama can walk into an eating establishment and order a plate teeming with grits, country sausage, and cornbread, wash it down with a glass full of iced sweet tea, and top it off with a slice of pecan pie.

But will that order be as good as a plateful of Southern deliciousness back home in Montgomery, Alabama? The jury is still out on that question.

One thing's for sure, though: Southern food is more popular than ever, in part thanks to Southern chefs who have starred in their own television cooking shows and have introduced the likes of chicken and dumplings, okra and tomatoes, and homemade biscuits to countless folks who may not have heard of such.

Imagine the expressions on the media folk who heard former professional football player Bruce Smith say this about Southern fare: "The most I ever ate? In one sitting? Maybe four big plates of fried chicken, biscuits, chitlins, gravy. Then dessert. Apple pie, sweet potato pie. My mother cooked that stuff, good Southern food, and when I was 300 pounds, I never missed a meal."

Southern cooking had its beginnings with Native Americans who introduced dishes such as grits and Brunswick stew to the colonists. As the region developed, each area adopted its own variety of culinary delights, ranging from Cajun and Creole in Louisiana to different styles of barbecue in the Carolinas, Tennessee, and Virginia. Mix in a bit of African influence, and soul food arrived in the South.

If you order tea in the South, don't expect a cup of hot tea. Down South it's iced sweet tea, or if you prefer something that will make your lips not pucker as much, simply request "half and half." The server will pour you half sweet tea and half unsweet (not cream), which is sometimes called half and half.

If you choose a soft drink down South, you have plenty from which to choose. Most of the popular sodas or pop (as those not from the region might say) were developed in the South. Think Coca-Cola, Pepsi, Dr. Pepper, RC Cola, and Mountain Dew, all Southern-born.

Cocktails synonymous with the South include mint juleps and Flaming Hurricanes. Kentucky is famous for bourbon, including a label called Southern Comfort, and Tennessee is home to Jack Daniel's whiskey, which is well known throughout the world.

* * *

I'm from Georgia, and everybody gathers around food in the South.

—Zac Brown, musician

It's as if we spend our entire lives avoiding Jell-O but it is always there at the end, waiting.

—John Grisham, author *Ford County*

The Southerner's ideal tomato sandwich—with a juicy, ripe tomato and the requisite amount of mayonnaise—will, when bitten into, send a stream of tomato juice and mayo out of the sandwich and down your arms. That's why you can't wear long sleeves. It's also why you stand over the sink, so the juice can run down your arms and drip from your elbows, safely, into the drain. When you're finished eating, just grab the soap, wash your arms and hands, and then go on about your day, happy in the knowledge that you have made and eaten a tomato sandwich just as your grandmama intended.

—Chuck Reece, author, "The Bitter Southerner"

I grew up in North Carolina, and they have a soft drink called Sun Drop. I love the diet version of it. It's the greatest thing on the face of the earth. I always have it in my fridge—bus fridge and home fridge.

—Eric Church, musician

How do you like yer possum, Lowell? Fallin' off the bones tender or with a little fight left in it?

      —Irene Ryan as Granny, *The Beverly Hillbillies*

Pecans are not cheap, my hons. In fact, in the South, the street value of shelled pecans just before holiday baking season is roughly that of crack cocaine. Do not confuse the two. It is almost impossible to make a decent crack cocaine tassie, I am told.

      —Celia Rivenbark, writer

Food is a way to explore culture and ground the story in a specific time and place. I still remember the meals and snacks from my first novel, *Shug*: pork chops and applesauce and Coca-Cola and peanuts, which are very Southern.

      —Jenny Han, author

I think I'm a lot like other moms out there who feel like if we don't have the pecan pie we have every year, then it just won't be Christmas.

      —Faith Hill, singer

She cooked by instinct, memory, and feel, from scenes and stories, from riverbanks, hog killings, and squirrel hunts. She learned to bake the perfect biscuit as her sister's first child was born, taught by her brother-in-law, a Navy man. She learned Brunswick stew beside a bonfire on the Coosa, just before a gathering of drunken men settled a feud with a hawk-billed knife. Such people will not eat dull food any more than they will tolerate a dull story.

—Rick Bragg, writer, talking about his
mother in *Southern Living* magazine

My grandmother on my mother's side, Granny, was a hairdresser. We would always go to her house for Sunday suppers. My grandmother wouldn't make the cornbread before she saw us on the inside of her door. Everything would be on the stove—she had been cooking slowly all day—but we couldn't eat because we had to wait for the cornbread. Then it would come out golden brown. Crispy around the edges. Just a bit of butter. It was just so good.
—Carla Hall, in an interview in *Garden & Gun*

I love raw cookie dough, right out of the tube. The other thing I eat is marshmallow fluff.

—Sandra Bullock, actress

You might be a redneck if you think that beef jerky and
Moon Pies are two of the major food groups.
—Jeff Foxworthy, humorist and author

Yeah, I like my rice and gravy and my black-eyed peas
Corn on the cob, I want a big glass of tea
Some okra and tomatoes and some turnip greens
I want some real soul food, do you know what I mean?
—Kenny Bill Stinson, "Taters and Gravy
and Chicken-Fried Steak"

Next to jazz music, there is nothing
that lifts the spirit and strengthens the
soul more than a good bowl of chili.
—Harry James, musician

No oyster in the world tastes as good as a Gulf oyster.
—Steve Scalise, US congressman from Louisiana

The only way that I could figure they could improve upon
Coca-Cola, one of life's most delightful elixirs, which
studies prove will heal the sick and occasionally raise the
dead, is to put bourbon in it.
—Lewis Grizzard, humorist, author,
and newspaper columnist

I've always wanted to throw a party where everyone comes with their mother's meatloaf. Everybody could evoke their mother's memory through her meatloaf.

—Diane Sawyer, journalist

One thing my mom taught me was that when you're making deviled eggs, flip the eggs over the night before. They've been sitting in the carton as they're transported, so the yolks settle on bottom. If you flip them, then the yolks aren't skewed to one side.

—Trisha Yearwood, singer and cookbook author

A Georgia peach, a real Georgia peach, a backyard great-grandmother's orchard peach, is as thickly furred as a sweater, and so fluent and sweet that once you bite through the flannel, it brings tears to your eyes.

—Melissa Faye Greene, author, *Praying for Sheetrock*

Man who invented the hamburger was smart; man who invented the cheeseburger was a genius.

—Matthew McConaughey, actor

Ham held the same rating as the basic black dress. If you had a ham in the meat house, any situation could be faced.

—Edna Lewis, chef and author

I'm good at anything that's country—biscuits, gravy, chicken-fried steak. Look at me, for God's sake. I cook what I like to eat.

—Blake Shelton, singer

Families need to have a time when they can cook together. They can eat at the table and you can look eye to eye. Phones are put away and there are no interruptions. And what you do is concentrate on each other. Listen to what they have to say, and let them listen to you.
—Kay Robertson, TV personality and cookbook author

Even during the rationing period, during World War II, we didn't have the anxiety that we'd starve, because we grew our own potatoes, you know? And our own hogs, and our own cows and stuff, you know.

—James Earl Jones, actor

I'm Southern, so alligator tail is pretty interesting and yummy.

—LeAnn Rimes, singer

Hunger gnawed at her empty stomach again and she said aloud: "As God is my witness, and God is my witness, the Yankees aren't going to lick me. I'm going to live through this, and when it's over, I'm never going to be hungry again. No, nor any of my folks. If I have to steal or kill—as God is my witness, I'm never going to be hungry again."

—Margaret Mitchell, author, *Gone with the Wind*

Let me be the first to tell you, drinking alcohol is the worst thing to do in cold weather. Hot soup is the best because the process of digesting food helps to warm you up.

—Morgan Freeman, actor

With the exception of octopus, I don't think I've met any food that I didn't like. And by the way, sometimes I do like octopus. I'm just not crazy about it by itself. I love sea urchin. I love uni. If I'm going to die of anything, it's going to be gluttony.

—Justin Timberlake, singer

Avoid fried foods, which angry up the blood.

Satchel Paige, former pitcher for the Cleveland Indians

When I'm home, I spend Sunday with my husband. If we're not cooking, we travel around in our camper, stop at fast-food restaurants, and picnic. We love that stuff that will harden your arteries in a hurry.

—Dolly Parton, singer and actress

I love a good breakfast—grits and eggs, French toast, turkey bacon. My grandmother on my father's side used to make tea cakes, and her breakfasts were unbelievable. There was fresh ham, and she would go out to the yard to get fresh eggs. She lived in rural Louisiana, and we'd spend summers with her.

—Tyler Perry, actor

There is a tradition in Southern cooking of recipes handed down for generations. And when I make my grandmother's strawberry pie—she is gone on now—I feel her right with me.

—Kimberly Schlapman, singer

After a hard day of basic training, you could eat a rattlesnake.

—Elvis Presley, singer

I'm from South Georgia, so my mom, she always cooked some dang good food when I was growing up.

—Phillip Phillips, singer, winner of the eleventh season of television's *American Idol*

You don't need a silver fork to eat good food.

—Paul Prudhomme, chef and restaurateur

The fact is that it takes more than ingredients and technique to cook a good meal. A good cook puts something of himself into the preparation— he cooks with enjoyment, anticipation, spontaneity, and he is willing to experiment.
—Pearl Bailey, author, *Pearl's Kitchen: An Extraordinary Cookbook*

The South, to me, is fried chicken and catfish caviar—that's grits—and good-looking women.
—Erk Russell, former football coach at Georgia Southern University

Ice cream was my undoing, and six chocolate milk shakes in a row were nothing to me at one time.
—Kate Smith, singer

CHAPTER 5

Let's Play Ball, Y'all

Cooperative weather makes the South the perfect back-drop for outside sports all year round. Residents from the Northeast and Midwest—where the weather often is freezing and sloppy during the winter months—tend to move to states below the Mason–Dixon line to retire or escape the cold weather so they can play golf and/or tennis.

Many of those residents are attracted to Southern communities built on and around golf and tennis facilities. Instead of driving to play their sport of choice, these Southerners can simply hop in their golf carts to take them to nearby courses or courts.

The most popular sport in the South, however, is college football. Can you yell "Roll Tide" (for the University of Alabama) or "War Eagle" (for Auburn University)? The region is home to colleges in the popular Southeastern Conference (SEC), the Atlantic Coast Conference (ACC), and the Big 12 Conference, where average attendance at a game can exceed 100,000.

In fact, college football games in the South have become somewhat of a cultural event. Die-hard fans make a Saturday-afternoon or night game a weekend event. They wear clothes in school colors, pack all kinds of food into their sport utility vehicles, and literally raise the tailgate for feasts on campus. At these gatherings—appropriately nicknamed "tailgates"—fans set out their favorite dishes on tables likely covered with tablecloths. Typically, a Southern tailgate might include spicy

Bloody Marys, refreshing mimosas (made with Florida orange juice), ice-cold beer straight out of the cooler, and finger foods such as hot wings, cheese straws, and chips and dip. However, some fans go all out and plan a spread straight out of the pages of *Southern Living* magazine. For Louisiana State University fans, for example, the magazine suggests: "Chicken and Sausage Gumbo, Potato Salad, Muffuletta Dip, Bayou Fried Shrimp with Remoulade Sauce, and Pecan Pralines."

While sampling the fare, imbibing on adult beverages, and cutting the fool under tents, fans will prepare for the upcoming game by switching on recordings of team songs. On autumn Saturdays, tunes such as "Rocky Top," "Glory, Glory," and Geaux Tigers" blare out of speakers at college tailgates throughout the South.

Depending on what team their school is playing, a fan might share a few jokes that will make their fellow tailgaters slap their knees and let out a hoot and a holler. These SEC jokes—certain to send readers into a laughing fit—were included in a *Sports Illustrated* magazine article by Fritz Lidz: "How many college students does it take to screw in a lightbulb?" At South Carolina it takes 80,000; one to screw in the bulb and 79,999 to discuss how this will finally be the year that they have a decent football team. At Alabama it takes five; one to change it, three to reminisce about how Bear Bryant would have done it, and one to throw the old bulb at an NCAA investigator. At Auburn it takes 100; one to screw in the bulb, 49 to talk about how they do it better than 'Bama, and 50 to realize it's all a lie, get looped, and roll Toomer's Corner. At Ole Miss it takes six; one to change the bulb, two to mix the drinks, and three to find the perfect J. Crew outfit to wear for the occasion.

Professional football also creates a big fan base in the South. Loyalists either tune in to games on TV or hightail it to the stadiums to watch the Atlanta Falcons, the New Orleans Saints, the Houston Oilers, the Miami Dolphins, the Dallas Cowboys, the Tennessee Titans, the Carolina Panthers, the Jacksonville Jaguars, and the Tampa Bay Buccaneers.

Almost before football season ends, basketball fever spreads to those living in several large Southern cities. Fanatic college fans cheer their hearts out, particularly at basketball-crazy universities like those in North Carolina, Virginia, and Kentucky. Pro teams include the Miami Heat, the New Orleans Pelicans, and a handful of others.

At one time baseball was even more popular than basketball and football in the South. Sprinkled throughout the region are minor league teams with colorful names such as the Durham (North Carolina) Bulls, the Augusta (Georgia) Green Jackets, and the Birmingham (Alabama) Barons. Major League Baseball teams include the Atlanta Braves, the Houston Astros, the Texas Rangers, the Miami Marlins, and the Tampa Bay Rays. Additionally, Florida is home to spring training camps for several MLB squads.

When it comes to professional golf, the South hosts several tournaments, including the Tournament Players Championship in Florida and the Masters, of course, in Georgia, part of the Grand Slam of golf. Professional golfer Bubba Watson had this to say when he won the Masters: "It's a dream come true for Bubba Watson from Bagdad, Florida, to have the green jacket on." The Ladies Professional Golf Association is headquartered in Florida and also schedules tourneys throughout the South.

The Daytona International Speedway in Florida is home to the National Association for Stock Car Racing (NASCAR), which enjoys an intense following in the South and throughout the United States. Each year NASCAR races are held in Atlanta, Charlotte, Talladega (Alabama), and Richmond, among other cities.

Not to be outdone, soccer has become popular at both the youth and collegiate levels. Professional soccer clubs can be found in Dallas, Houston, San Antonio, Orlando, and Atlanta.

Beachgoers throughout the South are known to play horseshoes, bocce, and a game called half rubber, which originated in my hometown of Savannah, Georgia. Equipment includes a rubber ball that is cut in half and a broom or mop handle used as a bat.

* * *

I came here to tell you one thing: come race time tomorrow, I'm coming for you.

—Ricky Bobby, *Talladega Nights: The Ballad of Ricky Bobby*

Close don't count in baseball. Close only counts in horseshoes and grenades.

—Frank Robinson, former outfielder for the Cincinnati Reds

No one will ever have golf under his thumb. No round ever will be so good it couldn't have been better. Perhaps this is why golf is the greatest of games. You are not playing a human adversary; you are playing a game. You are playing old man par.

—Bobby Jones, professional golfer

The regular season is where you make your name, but the postseason is where you make your fame.

—Walt Frazier, former professional basketball player for the New York Knicks

So, I didn't say we are going to win a lot, but we are going to play like winners, and we've got a plan in place to teach our guys how to play like winners and play like a champion.

—Steve Spurrier, former football coach for the University of Florida

When I was forty, my doctor advised me that a man in his forties shouldn't play tennis. I heeded his advice carefully and could hardly wait until I reached fifty to start again.

—Hugo Black, former associate justice
of the US Supreme Court

If you're going to play high school football, you do it in Texas or Florida or Georgia for the simple fact it's such a big deal.

—J. R. Martinez, actor

I guess there is nothing that will get your mind off everything like golf. I have never been depressed enough to take up the game, but they say you get so sore at yourself you forget to hate your enemies.

—Will Rogers, humorist and actor

It was electric. When Death Valley is rocking, it seems as if it might actually take flight. On Saturday, I went back to Baton Rouge to see Alabama barely beat LSU, and was, once again, reminded that Tiger Stadium is the best place in the world to watch a sporting event. . . . I'm not sure what it was like to walk into the Coliseum, but I bet it was something like this.

—Wright Thompson, journalist

I had started law school at Florida State University as a part-timer. I would go two quarters, and they allowed me to drop out to play baseball, and then I'd get readmitted in September. I was convinced I was going to be a lawyer and was using my baseball salary to pay my way through school.

—Tony La Russa, former manager of the Oakland Athletics

When I was a little bitty boy, I was a fan of boxing. But in Louisiana, it's football, football, football, and then everything else.

—James Carville, political commentator
and media personality

Opening day. All you have to do is say the words and you feel the shutters thrown wide, the room air out, the light pour in. In baseball, no other day is so pure with possibility. No scores yet, no losses, no blame or disappointment. No hangover—at least until the game's over.

—Mary Schmich, columnist for the *Chicago Tribune*

I don't care who you are, you're going to choke in certain matches. You get to a point where your legs don't move and you can't take a deep breath. You start to hit the ball about a yard wide, instead of inches.

—Arthur Ashe, former professional tennis player

That smell of freshly cut grass makes me think of Friday night football in high school. The smell of popcorn and cigar smoke reminds me of the stadium. The cutting of the grass reminds me of the August practice.

—Garth Brooks, singer

Oh, we played about, like, three tons of buzzard puke this afternoon.

—Spike Dykes, former football coach at Texas Tech

You win some, lose some, and wreck some.

—Dale Earnhardt, professional race-car driver

You know a lot of times wrestlers get too full of themselves. They can't separate themselves from the characters. They get used to the excitement, the energy, the lifestyle and the money, and with a lot of these guys, when it stops, they self-destruct.

—Hulk Hogan, former professional wrestler

If my mother put on a helmet and shoulder pads and a uniform that wasn't the same as the one I was wearing, I'd run over her if she was in my way. And I love my mother.

—Bo Jackson, author, *Bo Knows Bo: The Autobiography of a Ball Player*

When you're on a golf course, a couple of things are very interesting. No matter who you're with and who you're playing with, people want each other to do well.
—Condoleezza Rice, former US secretary of state

I'm from West Virginia. If you didn't know what was happening in NASCAR, you were on the outside. NASCAR is a big league sport, but it's still also country and redneck.
—Randy Moss, former professional football player

Old ballparks are like cathedrals in America. We don't have big old Gothic cathedrals like they do in Europe. But we got baseball parks.
—Jimmy Buffett, singer

I shall never forget my first visit to the property which is now Augusta National. The long lane of magnolias through which we approached was beautiful. The old manor house was charming. The rare trees and shrubs of the old nursery were enchanting. But when I walked out on the grass terrace under the big trees behind the house and looked down over the property, the experience was unforgettable. It seemed the land had been lying there for years just waiting for someone to lay a golf course upon it.
—Bobby Jones, former professional golfer

When I began playing the game, baseball was about as gentlemanly as a kick in the crotch.

—Ty Cobb, former professional baseball player

My dad was a high school basketball coach, so I was raised as a coach's son, and I was a baseball player back in Arkansas, and I lived in Texas, too, so I was just surrounded by sports. So that's what I was going to do: pitch for the St Louis Cardinals. I had no idea I was going to be an actor. So I got my collarbone broken in the Kansas City Royals training camp. And once I got hurt I started doing other things for a while.

—Billy Bob Thornton, actor

Only a man who knows what it is like to be defeated can reach down to the bottom of his soul and come up with the extra ounce of power it takes to win when the match is even.

—Muhammad Ali, former professional boxer

I remember the last season I played. I went home after a ball game one day, lay down on my bed, and tears came to my eyes. How can you explain that? It's like crying for your mother after she's gone. You cry because you love her. I cried, I guess, because I loved baseball, and I knew I had to leave it.

—Willie Mays, former center fielder
for the San Francisco Giants

I want to thank the NBA and USA Basketball. Words can't describe my feeling. I was a small-town kid from Hamburg, Arkansas, and you provided me a platform to live out my passion, the game of basketball, on the world's grandest stage.

—Scottie Pippen, former professional
basketball player for the Chicago Bulls

I'm from Florida, and my family somehow is really into country music. We're all Southern in a way: My grandpa hunts, my uncle's, like, a redneck, and we're all NASCAR fans.

—Cassadee Pope, singer, 2012 winner
of television's *The Voice*

My favorite Saturday, outside any Saturday
that Louisiana State University plays
football, is the Kentucky Derby.
—James Carville, political commentator
and media personality

My whole family likes to play basketball. George II plays for his high school team and George III and George IV and George V are going to be good players. One day we're going to have a team and call it Georgetown.

—George Foreman, former professional boxer

I tried real hard to play golf, and I was so bad at it they would have to check me for ticks at the end of the round because I'd spent about half the day in the woods.

—Jeff Foxworthy, humorist and author

My grandma once told my mama, "The kid's walking crazy around the cornfield, talking to himself." I was calling ball games.

—Keith Jackson, former sports announcer

There is no doubt about precisely when folks began racing each other in automobiles. It was the day they built the second automobile.

—Richard Petty, professional race-car driver

You give up your childhood. You miss proms and games and high-school events, and people say it's awful . . . I say it was a good trade. You miss something, but I think I gained more than I lost.

—Mary Lou Retton, former Olympic gymnast

Clemson will never subsidize a sport where a man sits on his butt and goes backwards.

—Frank Howard, Clemson University football coach, on the sport of rowing

I was nicknamed Skeeter in Little League because I was small and fast, like a mosquito flying across the outfield.

—Skeet Ulrich, actor

When you take a year off from football, you come back for all the enjoyable moments. When you're not playing, you miss out on all the highs, but you also miss these disappointments. But I would rather be in the arena to be excited or be disappointed than not have a chance at all. That's football. That's why everybody plays it.

—Peyton Manning, former quarterback
for the Indianapolis Colts

I ain't afraid to tell the world that it didn't take school stuff to help a fella play ball.

—Shoeless Joe Jackson, former professional baseball player.

For me, the Mount Rushmore of greats would be Ric Flair, Dusty Rhodes, Hulk Hogan, Bruno Sammartino or Lou Thesz. You can do either one of them in that fourth spot. But I think Ric Flair is the greatest of all time. He's the greatest I've ever seen . . . on the mic and in the ring.

—Darius Rucker, singer

Belted. It's a long one, deep into left center. Back goes Gionfriddo, back, back, back, back . . . he makes a one-handed catch in front of the bullpen! Oh, doctor!

—Red Barber, longtime sports announcer
for the Brooklyn Dodgers

Golf is me and my buddies out having a good time, but most of all, golf is about me and my dad. Anytime I think of golf, I think about my dad. He taught me how to hit a golf ball, and he got me playing.

—Justin Timberlake, singer

I told somebody once, "You don't want the Herschel that plays football . . . babysitting your child. When I am competing, I am a totally different person."

—Herschel Walker, former professional football player

CHAPTER 6

Art, Music, and Literature with a Southern Accent

As defined by Merriam-Webster, culture is "the beliefs, customs, arts, etc., of a particular society, group, place or time; a particular society that has its own beliefs, ways of life, art, etc.; a way of thinking, behaving or working that exists in a place . . ."

Think about Southern-based literary classics such as *Gone with the Wind* or *To Kill a Mockingbird*, music like Ray Charles's "Georgia on My Mind," or live theater with actors portraying Porgy and Bess on Catfish Row in Charleston, South Carolina. Add to that the long list of festivals and events held annually throughout the South. The first festival that comes to mind will likely be Mardi Gras in New Orleans, but there are other lesser-known gatherings that attract both locals and tourists from all over. There's the Chitlin' Hoedown, the Crawfish Boil, the RC and Moon Pie Festival, the World Championship Cardboard Boat Races, the Moonshiners Reunion, the Wooly Worm Festival, and plenty of others. Who could forget the Redneck Rodeo and a weekend devoted to Scallywags?

Down south, it's all those and plenty more. Jason Latour explains Southern pride and culture this way in *Southern Bastards, Volume 3*: "Southern pride comes from what we've built together. In our music and art and innovation. In the people who honor us by taking our culture out into the world and celebrating it. It comes from people seeking us out, and flocking here to experience all that we know and love. We are all neighbors. We are all Southerners. This is OUR culture, and it means what WE choose it to mean . . ."

The South truly is a melting pot, because of folks from foreign countries who long ago fled their homes for one reason or another and headed to the United States to establish communities in every state in the region. Their customs were blended with others, and the flavor of the South was born.

Southern music history started before the Civil War, when African slaves sang their songs in the fields of the South. Additionally, Southerners take pride in their country music, ragtime, Southern rock, gospel, blue-grass, and jazz. Beach music is a style popularized in the Carolinas, and includes music that you can dance the shag to; in fact, the shag is the state dance of South Carolina. Bands perform beach music along Myrtle Beach, South Carolina's Grand Strand, and at various spots throughout the South.

I love beach music
I always have and I always will.
There ain't no other kind of music in the
world that gives me quite the thrill.
When I hear "Sixty Minute Man"
and "Walking Up a One-Way Street,"
he's "up on the roof," he's "under the boardwalk,"
"Summertime's calling me."
    —The Embers, "I Love Beach Music"

Southern literature was boosted in the 1920s when satirist H. L. Mencken criticized Southern writers for not painting an authentic picture of the South. His articles prompted writers such as Tennessee Williams, Robert Penn Warren, and others to respond enthusiastically in what became known as the Southern Renaissance.

Even colleges and universities have jumped on the Southern culture bandwagon. The University of Mississippi has a Center for the Study of Southern Culture that "emphasizes the interdisciplinary investigation and documentation of the South as a region of cultural, historical, geographical and demographic complexity," according to the center's mission statement.

Course offerings on various Southern topics routinely are included on semester and quarter schedules at schools throughout the region. A keen interest in the culture of the South also has spread to educational institutions in other parts of the country as well. Additionally, the popularity of Southern art also has reached beyond the Mason–Dixon line. For example, Chris Flesher of Tennessee has a collection at New York City's American Folk Art Museum.

* * *

The American South is an authentic American Culture. Maybe the last. The North is just a Casserole Culture—a tasteless vat of leftovers, frozen peas and stale crumbs.
  —Tim Heaton, *The Southerner's Guide to Surviving New York City: For Gentlepersons of All Civilized Countries*

A little bit south you've got Macon, Georgia—home of the Allman Brothers, the Marshall Tucker Band and Capricorn Records. And off to the west you've got Delta blues. Sprinkle Southern gospel over the top of that, and you're talking about where I came from. I loved all of that music.
  —Travis Tritt, singer

My folks met at the University of Oklahoma, in the theater department in the 1940s. They were married touring the country in *Cinderella* and *Snow White*. My mother was married in Cinderella's costume; the dwarves were the best men.
  —Ron Howard, actor and director

Rock was born in the South, so saying "Southern rock" is like saying "rock rock."
  —Duane Allman, musician

It is a rare American who does not have some story about
how music has made our lives richer and more interesting,
how it has changed our moods, brought out the best in our
character, and even sometimes helped us earn a living.
              —Lamar Alexander, US senator from Tennessee

Hollywood is run by people who sit up in
their executive office, who are not connected
to Mississippi, Alabama, Chicago, South
Carolina. They know nothing about that,
they don't go to church, and they make their
decisions about what they think is right.
—Steve Harvey, actor and game-show host

My story is how a kid that's born into really destitute
poverty on a little dirt road in Florida winds up in one of the
largest bands in history.
                              —Don Felder, musician

But, when I had this feeling and started painting sacred art,
as I had this feeling to do, then it come to me: My problem
is I'll get a lot of criticism, and another problem is my
work's not good enough to sell.
                              —Howard Finster, artist

Country music originates with the colloquial, rural aspects of white America. It's really, truly, rural white America's blues.

—Dwight Yoakam, singer

I went to college at the University of South Carolina and dropped out of chemistry, and to fill a class, the only spot they had left was a theater class. It was so annoying, but I took it, and then I thought it was the greatest thing; the most socially creative. I dropped out of school immediately and moved to New York to start acting. I was nineteen.

—Jonny Weston, actor

Live theater is just an incredibly powerful medium, and I think anyone who goes, whether they know about it or not, if they see something that sort of fits with them, it's kind of hard to deny that they had a good time.

—Harry Connick Jr., singer and actor

I used to do puppet theater and also mime and musical theater in Florida for competitions and festivals, which was great. I was very much involved in theater when I was in college.

—Wesley Snipes, actor

Music is life itself. What would this world be without good music? No matter what kind it is.

—Louis Armstrong, jazz musician

Any form of art is a form of power; it has impact, it can affect change—it can not only move us, it makes us move.

—Ossie Davis, actor

If you talk bad about country music, it's like saying bad things about my mamma. Them's fightin' words.

—Dolly Parton, singer

I think maybe I was instrumental in taking the stereotype out of the Southern actor in some ways. I would hope my legacy would be as a serious actor who told the truth and did parts based on the quality of the part and not necessarily the money.

Billy Bob Thornton, actor

Many Southern writers must have learned the art of storytelling from listening to oral tales. I did. It gave me the knowledge that the simplest incident can make a story.

—Erskine Caldwell, writer

So, we went from being an Athens band to being a Georgia band to being a Southern band to being an American band from the East Coast to being an American band, and now we're kind of an international phenomenon.

—Michael Stipe, singer for the band R.E.M

When I was ten, I did a play at the Henry Street Settlement Playhouse, Charles Fuller's first play. He went on to write *A Soldier's Story*, among other things. I realized, "Oh, I can be anything doing this."

—Laurence Fishburne, actor

I've always tried to defend the idea that the blues doesn't have to be sung by a person who comes from Mississippi, as I did.
—B. B. King, musician

When I was a teenager, I continued to visit imaginary places by spending all my free time at our local community theater. Whether I acted in a play or worked backstage, the world of Tennessee Williams or Shakespeare always seemed more real to me than the dreary life of high school.

—Mary Pope Osborne, author

I do mostly Southern landscapes. I do beautiful old barns that are falling down, and beautiful trees reflecting in the water. My lovely wife Dorothy and I travel quite a bit, so I take pictures of different things that inspire me to come home, when I come home here in North Carolina, into my art studio and paint these things.

—James Best, actor

If you want to be a singer, you've got to concentrate on it twenty-four hours a day. You can't be a well driller, too. You've got to concentrate on the business of entertaining and writing songs. Always think different from the next person. Don't ever do a song as you heard somebody else do it.

—Otis Redding, singer

Mardi Gras is the love of life. It is the harmonic convergence of our food, our music, our creativity, our eccentricity, our neighborhoods, and our joy of living. All at once.
—Chris Rose, writer

The Grand Ole Opry, to a country singer, is what Yankee Stadium is to a baseball player. Broadway to an actor. It's the top of the ladder, the top of the mountain. You don't just play the Opry; you live it.

—Bill Anderson, singer

The entire elementary school in Rotan, Texas, presented a theatrical production of *Snow White and the Seven Dwarfs*. And the part of Sneezy fell to me.

—Tommy Lee Jones, actor

If *Gone with the Wind* has a theme, it is that of survival. What makes some people come through catastrophes and others, apparently just as able, strong, and brave, go under? It happens in every upheaval. Some people survive; others don't. What qualities are in those who fight their way through triumphantly that are lacking in those that go under? I only know that survivors used to call that quality gumption. So I wrote about people who had gumption and people who didn't.

—Margaret Mitchell, writer

A note can be as small as a pin or as big as the world, it depends on your imagination.

—Thelonious Monk, jazz musician

Painting is a lot harder than pickin' cotton. Cotton's right there for you to pull off the stalk, but to paint, you got to sweat your mind.

—Clementine Hunter, folk artist

I used to work in the cotton fields a lot when I was young. There were a lot of African Americans working out there. A lot of Mexicans—the blacks and the whites and the Mexicans, all out there singing, and it was like an opera in the cotton fields, and I can still hear it in the music that I write and play today.

—Willie Nelson, singer

When my sister and I were kids, swimming down in Charleston, there was this pizza parlor that had this old Dixieland band play, and I just loved Louis Armstrong and the sound of his voice, and I got up there with the band and started singing Louis Armstrong songs when I was a kid. I have no idea why, but I did it and I loved it.

—Thomas Gibson, actor

The one thing that can solve most of our problems is dancing.

—James Brown, singer

It takes more talent to write music, but it takes more courage to write lyrics.
—Johnny Mercer, lyricist

I was a little boy singing sad songs, about nine or ten years old, in the woods. I listened to my voice coming back to me. It was as high as you could go. I dreamed of being famous as a singer when I was in those cotton fields. I wanted to see the world and meet people.

—Percy Sledge, singer

To become a classical ballerina, you have to move to New York when you're twelve or eleven, and that becomes your life. I just wanted to be good in my company in Charleston, and I wanted it to always be part of my life.

—Jennifer Garner, actress

Find one person in the audience and sing to them with all of your heart. And then cast a spell over them. Hoss, if you can't do it with feeling—don't.

—Patsy Cline, singer

Honey, I just decided you're depressed and need cheering up, so I'm going to give you a party.

—Truman Capote, author

Pilgrims travel to Jerusalem to see the Holy Land, and the foundations of their faith. People go to Washington, DC, to see the workings of government, and the foundation of our country. And fans flock to Nashville to see the foundation of country music, the Grand Ole Opry.

—Brad Paisley, singer

Country music is about new love and it's about old love.

—Jeff Foxworthy, comedian

I was this little kid living in the middle of nowhere in Arkansas. I found out really quickly that I didn't want to look at the south end of a northbound mule. Because of music, it's led to this incredible life.

—Glen Campbell, singer, in a 2011 interview with the *San Francisco Chronicle*

As a musician you have to keep one foot back in the past and have one foot forward into the future.

—Dizzy Gillespie, musician

I grew up in a small town in Alabama, and there wasn't much in the way of entertainment, so like our older siblings before us, we drove our pickup trucks out into the hayfield and lit a bonfire.

—Abbi Glines, author

We're definitely a hodgepodge of influences. Mine, most heavily, would be Southern rock—the Allman Brothers, Lynyrd Skynyrd and stuff like that. Hillary [Scott] is more from the country side—her mom is Linda Davis, a country singer. Dave [Haywood], he's a big fan of the Eagles and like that.

—Charles Kelley, musician, member of Lady Antebellum

I come to writing from hearing great stories as a child in Louisiana, where the mark of a person was his or her ability to be a raconteur. I also come to writing as a professional actress whose body has been trained to listen and smell and inhabit characters without judgment.

—Rebecca Wells, writer

Growing up I played piano and I sang at a lot of weddings;
I grew up in a very small town, a little coal-mining town in
Virginia called Grundy. And my family was very sing-songy
at home.

—Jayma Mays, actress

Somebody got the idea nobody didn't listen to my kinda
music. I told everybody on the radio that this was my last
program. "If anybody's enjoyed it," I said, "I'd like to
hear from 'em." I got four hundred cards and letters that
afternoon and the next mornin' . . . They decided they
wanted to keep my kind of music.

—Hank Williams, musician

When I was young, my family didn't go on
outings to the circus or trips to Disneyland.
We couldn't afford them. Instead, we
stayed in our small rural West Texas town,
and my parents took us to cemeteries.
—Jenny Lawson, journalist

I sang in church growing up. Memphis is the blues capital of
the world, we like to say.

—Justin Timberlake, singer

When she gets rattled, the South really comes out. Once when Daddy tried to cancel our country club membership because he said the dues were too high, she went from zero to Atlanta burning in zero point five seconds.

—Jen Lancaster, author, *Here I Go Again*

Busted flat in Baton Rouge
And headin' for the trains
Feelin' nearly faded as my jeans
Ol' Bobby thumbed a diesel down
Just before it rained
Lord, took us all the way to New Orleans.
And I pulled my harpoon out of my dirty red bandanna
Blowed it low while Bobby sang the blues
With them windshield wipers slappin' time
And Bobby clappin' hands with mine . . .

—Roger Miller, "Me and Bobby McGee"

I'm from Louisiana, and that's where I got my start, in Cajun music. There's a huge music scene down there centered around our culture. Those are people that are not making music for a living. They are making music for the fun of it. And I think that's the best way I could have been introduced to music.

—Hunter Hayes, musician

In that fall, in the blue twilights, girls came clicking home from their jobs in their clunky heels and miniskirts and opened their apartment windows to the winesap air, and got out ice cubes, and put on Petula Clark singing "Downtown," and sat down to wait. Soon the young men would come, drifting out of their bachelor apartments in Bermuda shorts and Top-Siders, carrying beers and gin and tonics, looking for a refill and a date and the keeping of promises that hung in the bronze air like fruit on the eve of ripeness.

—Anne Rivers Siddons, author, *Downtown*

When you begin to see the possibilities of music, you desire to do something good for people, to help humanity free itself from its hang-ups.
—John Coltrane, musician

CHAPTER 7

Civil Rights and Justice for All

The fight for civil rights for all in the South—especially African Americans—began brewing before slavery was abolished. After the Civil War, African Americans were still looked upon as lesser-class citizens. The focus on civil rights came to a head in 1954 when the US Supreme Court ruled on *Brown v. Board of Education of Topeka, Kansas*, agreeing that segregation in public schools is unconstitutional.

Nevertheless, Jim Crow was alive and well in the South and had been since Reconstruction days. Jim Crow is said to have been modeled after a fictitious character in a degrading minstrel show and was the name given to state and local laws that were enacted to enforce racial segregation. Under Jim Crow, African Americans in the South were not allowed to drink from the same public water fountains, sit in the same waiting rooms, or use the same restrooms as white people, among other laws.

A little progress on the national scene occurred in 1941 when President Franklin D. Roosevelt issued an executive order that opened government jobs to all Americans regardless of race, creed, color, or national origin. After World War II, President Harry Truman signed an executive order to end discrimination in the military.

Despite the strides made for civil rights—the Fifteenth Amendment, giving African Americans the right to vote, for one—African Americans continued to be slighted. In Alabama, for example, Jim Crow laws demanded that African Americans sit in the back of city buses and give up their seats to white passengers if the bus was full. In 1955, in Montgomery, a woman named Rosa Parks got on a bus and found a seat. When a white man got on and couldn't find a seat, the driver told Parks to vacate hers for the man. When Parks refused, she was arrested. As a result, she became the mother of the civil rights movement, and African-American community leaders, including the Reverend Martin Luther King Jr., established the Montgomery Improvement Association.

One of the first actions taken by the MIA was a boycott of the Montgomery bus system, which lasted more than a year. In 1956 the Supreme Court ruled that segregated seating was unconstitutional. In 1957 nine African-American students who became known as the Little Rock Nine arrived at Central High School and were turned away by angry protesters, as well as the Arkansas National Guard. The nine tried to attend classes again a couple of weeks later, but violence erupted once again. Finally, President Dwight D. Eisenhower ordered federal troops to escort the nine to and from classes. Eisenhower also signed the Civil Rights Act of 1957, which allowed federal prosecution of anyone who tried to prevent someone from voting.

Three years later, four African-American college students refused to leave a Woolworth's lunch counter in Greensboro, North Carolina, because they were refused service. Over the next few days, lunch-counter sit-ins popped up throughout the South, which led to the original four students being served.

On August 28, 1963, the March on Washington—organized by Asa Philip Randolph and others—took place. Beforehand, Randolph had explained the purpose of the march: "I suggest that 10,000 Negroes march on Washington, DC, the capital of the Nation, with the slogan, 'We loyal Negro American citizens demand the right to work and fight for our country.' "

It was in Washington that Martin Luther King Jr.'s "I Have a Dream" speech became one of the most iconic events in the civil rights movement. More than 200,000 people, black and white, congregated in Washington, DC, for the peaceful march, with the main purpose being to force civil rights legislation and establish job equality for everyone. The highlight of the march was King's speech, in which he said, in part: "I have a dream . . . that my four little children will one day live in a nation where they will not be judged by the color of their skin but by the content of their character," and the desire to "transform the jangling discords of our nation into a beautiful symphony of brotherhood . . . And when this happens . . . and when we allow freedom ring, when we let it ring from every village and every hamlet, from every state and every city, we will be able to speed up that day when all of God's children, black men and white men, Jews and Gentiles, Protestants and Catholics, will be able to join hands and sing in the words of the old Negro spiritual:

'Free at last! Free at last! Thank God Almighty, we are free at last!' "

The following year President Lyndon B. Johnson signed the Civil Rights Act of 1964, which guaranteed equal employment for all, limited the use of voter literacy tests, and allowed federal authorities to ensure that public facilities were integrated.

But civil rights battles were far from over. In Alabama on March 7, 1965, six hundred peaceful demonstrators participated in the Selma-to-Montgomery march to protest the killing of a black civil rights activist by a white police officer, and to encourage legislation to enforce the Fifteenth Amendment. They were beaten and tear-gassed by police, and the day became known as Bloody Sunday.

Years later journalist Jon Meacham wrote about the turbulent period: "As a Southerner born after the epic events of the civil rights movement, I've always wondered how on earth people of good will could have conceivably lived with Jim Crow—with the daily degradations, the lynchings in plain sight, and, as the movement gathered force, with the fire hoses and the police dogs and the billy clubs."

The era was due for even more violence and tragedy. On April 4, 1968, civil rights leader and Nobel Peace Prize recipient, King, was assassinated in Memphis, Tennessee. Within days, the Fair Housing Act was made into law, prohibiting housing discrimination based on race, sex, national origin, and religion.

Great strides were made on the home front when Barack Obama, an African-American resident of Chicago, became the forty-fourth president of the United States in 2008. But even Obama couldn't halt the racial tensions that still exist in this country.

* * *

This Civil Rights Act is a challenge to all of us to go to work in our communities and our states, in our homes and in our hearts, to eliminate the last vestiges of injustice in our beloved country. So tonight I urge every public official, every religious leader, every business and professional man, every working man, every housewife—I urge every American—to join in this effort to bring justice and hope to all our people, and to bring peace to our land.

—Lyndon B. Johnson, thirty-sixth
president of the United States

America is not perfect. It took a bloody civil war to free over four million African Americans who lived enslaved. It took another hundred years after that before they achieved full equality under the law.

—Marco Rubio, US senator from Florida

From politics and business to music and food to culture, African Americans have helped to shape our state's colorful past and its future.

> —Mary Landrieu, former US senator from Louisiana

I think that the thing that we learned back in the day of the civil rights movement is that you do have to keep on keeping on.

> —Charlayne Hunter-Gault, journalist and one of the first
> African Americans to attend the University of Georgia

People notice if you are black. People notice if you are female. We are certainly not either color-blind or gender-blind in this country, so I'm not suggesting that it isn't a factor. But I think in the final analysis, people will take a look at the positions, and they'll take a look at the issues.

> —Condoleezza Rice, sixty-sixth US secretary of state

I realize that I'm black, but I like to be viewed as a person, and this is everybody's wish.

> —Michael Jordan, professional basketball
> player for the Chicago Bulls

Let us look at Jim Crow for the criminal he is and what he has done to one life multiplied millions of times over these United States and the world. He walks us on a tightrope from birth.

> —Rosa Parks, activist

My version of "Georgia" became the state song of Georgia. That was a big thing for me, man. It really touched me. Here is a state that used to lynch people like me suddenly declaring my version of a song as its state song. That is touching.

—Ray Charles, musician

It's easy to forget history or give it a Cliff Notes. The Cliff Notes of history. But mainly, so much of what happens in *Eyes on the Prize* happened in Jackson, Mississippi. Jackson, Mississippi, isn't really known for any other touchstone to the movement, other than Medgar Evers being killed. There were sit-ins and riots and atrocities.

—Tate Taylor, actor

A color-blind society eludes us. For one reason, we have not sought diligently and contentiously to pursue it. It is one thing to mouth the words, but it is quite another to perform the deeds.

—John Hope Franklin, historian

The time will come when the Negro in the South will be accorded all the political rights which his ability, character, and material possessions entitle him to.

—Booker T. Washington, author, *A Will to Be Free*

In the summer of 1966, I went to Mississippi to be in the heart of the civil rights movement, helping people who had been thrown off the farms or taken off the welfare rolls for registering to vote. While working there, I met the civil rights lawyer I later married—we became an interracial couple.

—Alice Walker, writer

An activist is someone who makes an effort to see problems that are not being addressed and then makes an effort to make their voice heard. Sometimes there are so many things that it's almost impossible to make your voice heard in every area, but you can sure try.

—Joanne Woodward, actress

Racism separates, but it never liberates. Hatred generates fear, and fear, once given a foothold, binds, consumes and imprisons. Nothing is gained from prejudice. No one benefits from racism.

—Thurgood Marshall, former associate justice of the US Supreme Court

Touring a segregated America—forever being stopped and harassed by white cops—hurt you most because you don't realize the damage. You hold it in. You feel empty, like someone reached in and pulled out your guts. You feel hurt and dirty, less than a person.
—B. B. King, musician

There was never a time you could get the majority of people in Alabama or Mississippi, or even southern Delaware, to vote to end segregation. What changed things was the rule of law, the courts. *Brown v. Board of Education* was ushered in by a movement, but it was a legal decision.
—Bryan Stevenson, activist/attorney

Hating people because of their color is wrong. And it doesn't matter which color does the hating. It's just plain wrong.
—Muhammad Ali, late professional boxer

Shaking hands with the Queen of England was a long way from being forced to sit in the colored section of the bus going into downtown Wilmington, North Carolina.
—Althea Gibson, former professional tennis player

I think young people don't really know that much about the civil rights movement and about the history of African Americans in this country. It's not taught enough in school.
—Don Lemon, journalist

I got agitated at the idea that racism is a Southern thing. Did you hear about the cross burning out here? A black family moved into an upper-middle-class Los Angeles suburb and found a cross burning on their lawn. Swastikas are being painted on synagogues. I'm moving to France. I don't think this "kinder, gentler nation" bit is working too well.
—Pruitt Taylor Vince, actor

On matters of race, South Carolina has a tough history. We all know that. Many of us have seen it in our own lives—in the lives of our parents and our grandparents. We don't need reminders.
—Nikki Haley, former South Carolina governor and US ambassador to the United Nations

I am a planter—a cotton planter. I am a Southern man and a slaveholder—a kind and a merciful one, I trust—and none the worse for being a slaveholder.
—John C. Calhoun, politician

We're not thought of in terms of color because we are entertainers. We are there to entertain you not because we are black, white, pink, or green, or gay or straight, or because we are Catholic or Protestant.

—Eartha Kitt, actress

Early on, I was so impressed with Charles Dickens. I grew up in the South, in a little village in Arkansas, and the whites in my town were really mean, and rude. Dickens, I could tell, wouldn't be a man who would curse me out and talk to me rudely.

—Maya Angelou, poet and activist

Never be afraid to raise your voice for honesty and truth and compassion against injustice and lying and greed. If people all over the world . . . would do this, it would change the earth.

—William Faulkner, writer

Whenever I hear protests from the South that it should be left alone to deal with the Negro question, my thoughts go back to that scene of brutality and savagery. I do not see how a people that can find in its conscience any excuse whatever for slowly burning to death a human being, or for tolerating such an act, can be entrusted with the salvation of a race.

—James Weldon Johnson, *The Autobiography of an Ex-Colored Man*

I refuse to accept the view that mankind is so tragically
bound to the starless midnight of racism and war that
the bright daybreak of peace and brotherhood can never
become a reality . . . I believe that unarmed truth and
unconditional love will have the final word.

> —Martin Luther King Jr., pastor and activist

That's part of American greatness, is discrimination. Yes,
sir. Inequality, I think, breeds freedom and gives a man
opportunity.

> —Lester Maddox, former governor of Georgia

The absolute worst I have ever been treated, the worst
things that have been done to me, the worst things that have
been said about me, are by Northern liberal elites, not by
the people of Savannah, Georgia.

> —Clarence Thomas, associate justice
> of the US Supreme Court

An American should be able to choose to work in a place
where he is with his kind of people and not find that at the
counters, desks, or benches they will be forced to work,
side by side, with all types of people of all races; that in
the lunchrooms, restrooms, recreation rooms, they will be
compelled by law to mingle with persons and races which
all their lives they have, by free choice, avoided in social and
business intercourse.

> —Strom Thurmond, former US senator from South Carolina

Every time I look at my pocketbook, I see Jackie Robinson.
                              —Willie Mays, former center fielder
                              for the San Francisco Giants

I chose as my target the University of Mississippi, which
in 1960 was the holiest temple of white supremacy in
America, next to the US Capitol and the White House, both
of which were under the control of segregationists and their
collaborators.
                              —James Meredith, activist

Why would we have different races if God meant us to be
alike and associate with each other?
                              —Lester Maddox, former governor of Georgia

Many people resented my impatience and
honesty, but I never cared about acceptance
as much as I cared about respect.
—Jackie Robinson, former second
baseman for the Brooklyn Dodgers

There is racism all over the United States. Most
Southerners I know, we definitely find ourselves defending
our heritage.
                              —Octavia Spencer, actress

I draw the line in the dust and toss the gauntlet before the feet of tyranny, and I say segregation now, segregation tomorrow, segregation forever.

—George Wallace, former governor of Alabama

No race can prosper till it learns that there is as much dignity in tilling a field as in writing a poem.

—Booker T. Washington, educator

Jim Crow is alive and it's dressed in a Brooks Brothers suit, my friend, instead of a white robe.

—Myrlie Evers-Williams, activist

I know my destiny. I was born into animosity, bigotry and hatred. We had water for white folks, and water for colored folks. White lines, black lines. I came from Beaufort in South Carolina, and it was tougher than Georgia, Alabama and Mississippi.

—Joe Frazier, former professional boxer

CHAPTER 8

It Ain't Called the Bible Belt for Nothin'

The South, like most regions in the United States, is a mixture of religious denominations—Protestant, Catholic, Jewish, Muslim, and plenty of others.

But it probably comes as no surprise to anyone who knows anything that the South is part of the area in the country known as the Bible Belt, or the area in which Southern Baptists, Methodists, and evangelical Christians are the predominant religious groups. The term was first used in 1925 by journalist H. L. Mencken when he was covering the Scopes Monkey Trial in Tennessee. Today the Bible Belt region stretches from northern Texas to western North Carolina, and from Mississippi north to Kentucky.

Critics of worshippers who live in the Bible Belt have been known to label them Bible thumpers and holy rollers, among other derogatory terms. Outsiders (and some insiders) tend to view Southern religious folks as over-the-top conservative, and there may be some truth to that theory. Singer-songwriter Kacey Musgraves disagrees: "My parents aren't crazy conservative. They're actually pretty open-minded. But my grandparents are, and where I'm from, East Texas, is the Bible Belt."

In the 1970s, the core of the Bible Belt—or the buckle where most of the Baptist, Pentecostal, and fundamentalist congregations were located—was in eastern Tennessee. By 2000, the buckle had moved to north-central Texas and southwestern Oklahoma.

The number of faithful who attend Baptist churches in various Southern states is astonishing. In 2014, for example, New Spring Community Church in Anderson, South Carolina, had an average Sunday attendance of more than 27,000. That same year the Second Baptist Church in Houston averaged 26,000 each Sunday.

Baptists, Methodists and fundamentalist denominations certainly aren't the only congregations in the South. Judaism has a high percentage of followers in Charleston, South Carolina, for example, and in other parts of the region.

For people that aren't familiar with Jewish life in the South, I think the temptation is to think in clichés or tokenization, like: "Oh what a quirky thing, there are communities in Alabama. Who'd have thunk? But for the Jews down here, this is their life. They don't see themselves as a novelty. This is part of the American Jewish experience, and it's a part, unfortunately, that's not told accurately or often enough.

—Rabbi Jeremy Simons, staff rabbi of
the Institute of Jewish Life

Catholicism also is part of the Southern landscape. In 2000 the US Census Bureau counted 1.4 million Catholics in Louisiana, mostly in the southern part of the state, because of French and Spanish heritage.

Moreover, historic African-American congregations—many established by former slaves—are sprinkled throughout the South. Membership in African Methodist Episcopal churches increased after Reconstruction.

Prominent Southern writers often included religious themes in their works. William Faulkner, Carson McCullers, and Flannery O'Connor, who was a devout Catholic, often were asked about the religious themes in their writings. O'Connor said this: "Even in the life of a Christian, faith rises and falls like the tides of an invisible sea. It's there, even when he can't see it or feel it, if he wants it to be there. You realize, I think, that it is more valuable, more mysterious, altogether more immense than anything you can learn or decide upon. It will keep you free—not free to do anything you please, but free to be formed by something larger than your own intellect or the intellects around you."

Like O'Connor, William Faulkner grew up observing religion in the South, and included references (like the following, from *The Best of Faulkner*) in many of his books: "He had a word, too. Love, he called it. But I had been used to words for a long time. I knew that that word was like the others: just a shape to fill a lack; that when the right time came, you wouldn't need a word for that any more than for pride or fear . . . One day I was talking to Cora. She prayed for me because she believed I was blind to sin, wanting me to kneel and pray too, because people to whom sin is just a matter of words, to them salvation is just words too."

*   *   *

The church is God saying: "I'm throwing a banquet, and all these mismatched, messed-up people are invited. Here, have some wine."
> —Rachel Held Evans, author, *Searching for Sunday: Loving, Leaving, and Finding the Church*

I don't appreciate a preacher who commits adultery and then goes out and blames me.
> —Jimmy Swaggart, televangelist

As long as algebra is taught in school, there will be prayer in school.
> —Cokie Roberts, journalist

My brother and I have converted to Christianity, and my other brother and sister are still Sikh. So for me, it's not something that I ever want to be judgmental on. I know my parents are two people of a very strong faith. I respect all that they've done in raising their four kids and in the opportunities that they've given us.
> —Nikki Haley, former governor of South Carolina and former US ambassador to the United Nations

What I miss today more than anything else—I don't go to church as much anymore—but that old-time religion, that old singing, that old praying which I love so much. That is the great strength of my being, of my writing.

—Ernest Gaines, writer

I lived in a project and . . . didn't have a good education. But . . . I'd listen to the preacher, who said that God would show me the way. Everything starts from that confidence.
—Evander Holyfield, former professional boxer

We need to be clear in calling out evil for what it is. When people will behead a child, and when people will leave people starving on top of a mountain without food or water—40,000 of them—I don't care what religion it is: It's evil.

—Mike Huckabee, former governor of Arkansas

I was always going to church with my mom, dad and sister. I was literally raised under the godly influence both at home and church. There was no alcohol and no smoking at our house. That was the way a Bowden was supposed to live. My dad always told me to represent the Bowden name in a respectful manner.

—Bobby Bowden, former football coach
for Florida State University

I guess it is what you do if you grow up with warnings of damnation ringing from every church door and radio station and family reunion, in a place where total strangers will walk up to you at the Piggly Wiggly and ask if you are Saved. Even if you deny that faith, rebuke it, you still carry it around with you like some half-forgotten Indian head penny you keep in your pocket for luck. I wonder sometimes if I will be the same, if when I see my life coming to an end I will drop to my knees and search my soul for old sins and my memory for forgotten prayers. I reckon so.

—Rick Bragg, author, *All Over But the Shoutin'*

I'm a Frisbeetarian. We worship Frisbees. We believe when you die your soul goes up on the roof and you can't get it down.

—Jim Stafford, singer

Christianity is being concerned about [others], not building a million-dollar church while people are starving right around the corner. Christ was a revolutionary person, out there where it was happening. That's what God is all about, and that's where I get my strength.

—Fannie Lou Hamer, activist

I am and always will be a sinner. But that's the beautiful thing about Jesus. I'll always try to be a better person in the eyes of God. But I'm not all of a sudden stepping up on a pedestal and saying I'm holier than thou, 'cause I'm not!

—Billy Ray Cyrus, singer

Well don't you expect me to come to one of your churches or one of those tent-revivals with all those Bible-beaters doin' God-only-knows-what! They'd probably make me eat a live chicken!

—Shirley MacLaine as Ouiser, *Steel Magnolias*

I was raised in a little church, the Grundy Methodist Church, that was very straight-laced, but I had a friend whose mother spoke in tongues. I was just wild for this family. My own parents were older, and they were so overprotective. I just loved the "letting go" that would happen when I went to church with my friend.

—Lee Smith, author

After I released "Jesus, Take the Wheel," people started saying, Oh, it's kind of risky. You're coming out with a religious song. And I was thinking, Really? I grew up in Oklahoma; I always had a close relationship with God. I never thought it was risky in the least. If anything, I thought it was the safest thing I could do.

—Carrie Underwood, singer

The scripture is God's plan on how we are to live our lives here and what we are to do to have eternal life.
—Deborah Norville, journalist

When you have God behind you, you can come out on top every time.

—Alvin C. York, one of the most decorated soldiers in World War I

Jehovah's Witness are welcomed into my home . . . You gotta respect anybody who gets all dressed up in Sunday clothes and goes door-to-door on days so hot their high heels sink a half-inch into the pavement. The trick is to do all the talking yourself. Pretty soon, they'll look at their watches and say, Speaking of end times, wouldja look at what time it is now!

—Celia Rivenbark, writer

I would rather be a servant in the House of the Lord than to sit in the seats of the mighty.
—Alben W. Barkley, thirty-fifth vice president of the United States

Two of the central ingredients to our family are food and faith, so sitting down together and thanking God for the food He's provided means everything to us. Prayer is a natural part of our lives—not only around the dinner table but all day long.

—Phil Robertson, businessman

The day the squirrel went berserk
In the First Self-Righteous Church
In that sleepy little town of Pascagoula
It was a fight for survival that broke out in revival
They were jumpin' pews and shoutin' Hallelujah!

—Ray Stevens, "The Mississippi Squirrel Revival"

I pray every night, sometimes long prayers about a lot of things and a lot of people, but I don't talk about it or brag about it because that's between God and me, and I'm no better than anybody else in God's sight.

—Peyton Manning, former quarterback
for the Indianapolis Colts

I grew up in Nacogdoches, Texas . . . raised by my grandmother. We were very poor and had no indoor plumbing. My grandmother was a very religious woman, though, and she gave me a lot of faith and inner strength.

—Alana Stewart, actress

People see God every day; they just don't recognize him.

—Pearl Bailey, singer

Good preachers don't preach about God and heaven, and things like that. They always preach against something, like hell and the devil. Them is things to be against. It wouldn't do a preacher no good to preach for God. He's got to preach against the devil and all wicked and sinful things. That's what the people like to hear about. They want to hear about the bad things.

—Erskine Caldwell, author, *Tobacco Road*

I used to always sit in church looking out the windows at the boys, wondering if I could make an excuse to go out and, you know, go to the bathroom, because all the outdoor toilets. But anyhow, I was only going out to see the boys.
—Dolly Parton, singer

When I'm onstage, I'm trying to do one thing: bring people joy. Just like church does. People don't go to church to find trouble, they go there to lose it.

—James Brown, singer

Every day I wake up and I lay in bed counting my blessings and saying my prayers for how fortunate I am to have great fans and health and family.

—Luke Bryan, singer

The Devil went down to Georgia
He was lookin' for a soul to steal
He was in a bind 'cause he was way behind
He was willing to make a deal
When he came across this young man sawin' on a fiddle
and playin' it hot
And the Devil jumped up on a hickory stump
and said, Boy, let me tell you what.

—The Charlie Daniels Band, "The
Devil Went Down to Georgia"

I've never known more Jesus-serving, Jesus-loving, people-loving, people-serving folks on earth than right here in my hometown of Houston, Texas.

—Beth Moore, author

We think when God speaks to us, there's going to be a boom out of Heaven or we're going to get some chill bumps, but I really believe God's talking to us all the time. He's talking to us right in here. I call it our heart, our conscience, but it's the Holy Spirit talking to us.

—Joel Osteen, televangelist

I'm a firm believer in God himself, but that's as far as I can go. I'm not any denomination. I'm not Catholic or Presbyterian or Baptist or Methodist or Jewish or Muslim. I'm none of those things. And I'm sure that's just fine with God.

—Ray Charles, singer

Being a Baptist won't keep you from sinning, but it'll sure as hell keep you from enjoying it.

—Jimmy Dean, singer and businessman

The greatest legacy one can pass on to one's children and grandchildren is not money or other material things accumulated in one's life, but rather a legacy of character and faith.

—Billy Graham, evangelist

Faith is salted and peppered through everything at Christmas. And I love at least one night by the Christmas tree to sing and feel the quiet holiness of that time that's set apart to celebrate love, friendship, and God's gift of the Christ child.

—Amy Grant, singer

A church is a place in which gentlemen who have never been to heaven brag about it to persons who will never get there.

—H. L. Mencken, journalist

Religious faith is not a storm cellar to which men and women can flee for refuge from the storms of life. It is, instead, an inner spiritual strength which enables them to face those storms with hope and serenity.

—Sam Ervin, author, *Humor of a Country Lawyer*

I grew up in a very small, close-knit, Southern Baptist family, where everything was off-limits. So I couldn't wait to get to college and have some fun. And I did for the first two years. And I regret a lot of it, because my grades were in terrible shape. I never got in serious trouble, except for my grades.

—John Grisham, author

Faith is the strength by which a shattered world shall emerge into the light.
—Helen Keller, author

My mother was truly my saving grace, because she would take me to church with her. I would see my mother smiling in the choir, and I wanted to know this God that made her so happy. If I had not had that faith in my life, I don't know where I would be right now.

—Tyler Perry, actor

God has never disappointed me.

—Brenda Lee, singer

I think people who don't believe in God are crazy. How can you say there is no God when you hear the birds singing these beautiful songs you didn't make?

—Little Richard Penniman, singer

I think it is safe to say that while the South is hardly Christ-centered, it is most certainly Christ-haunted.

—Flannery O'Connor, author

As I was growing up, I did a lot of talent shows. I won fifteen Sunday nights straight in a series of talent shows in Macon. I showed up the sixteenth night, and they wouldn't let me go on anymore. Whatever success I had was through the help of the good Lord.

—Otis Redding, singer

Well, for me, I grew up very Southern Baptist, and I definitely lived in my bubble. You know, I lived in my bubble that was in my church.

—Jessica Simpson, actress

I am a Christian person, and I do love the Lord, and I feel no matter who you are, what you believe, how you live your life, it's not my place to judge. I don't have that power. I don't want that power. It's my place to love and to show God's love to other people, even if they don't live a life like I live.

—Carrie Underwood, singer

I grew up in a religious environment, and I'm proud of it. I was going to be a priest; I'm proud of it. And I thank God I believe in God, or I would probably be enormously angry right now.

—Clarence Thomas, associate justice
of the US Supreme Court

May the same wonder-working Deity, who long since delivered the Hebrews from their Egyptian oppressors, planted them in a promised land, whose providential agency has lately been conspicuous in establishing these United States as an independent nation, still continue to water them with the dews of heaven and make the inhabitants of every denomination participate in the temporal and spiritual blessings of that people whose God is Jehovah.

—George Washington, in a Letter to the Hebrew
Congregations of the City of Savannah, Georgia, May, 1789

Being human means you will make mistakes. And you will make mistakes, because failure is God's way of moving you in another direction.

—Oprah Winfrey, entertainer

I separated from the Southern Baptists when they adopted the discriminatory attitude towards women, because I believe what Paul taught in Galatians, that there is no distinction in God's eyes between men and women, slaves and masters, Jews and non-Jews—everybody is created equally in the eyes of God.

—Jimmy Carter, thirty-ninth president of the United States

CHAPTER 9

Loud and Proud Opinions

The South has played a key role in the nation's political arena for what seems like forever. In the early days of the country, founding fathers like George Washington, Thomas Jefferson, and the rest of the bunch seemed to be as political as they come, voicing their thoughts on this and that, whenever they could bend an ear, or twenty. That's the nature of politics, and it continues in the South today.

The Civil War brought out various types of Southern politicians. Men such as Jefferson Davis, who was president of the Confederate States of America, became household words.

For nearly a century after Reconstruction, the white South seemed to identify with the Democratic Party, but gradually turned Republican when Democrats began siding with liberal causes, according to former US senator Herman E. Talmadge of Georgia: "From 1948 on, the Democratic Party has moved to the left politically and to the north geographically."

The year 1948 was when a few Southern Democrats formed the States Rights Democratic Party (or Dixiecrats) that wanted to continue racial segregation in the region. South Carolina governor Strom Thurmond was the party's unsuccessful presidential nominee against Harry Truman. Thurmond did, however, carry Alabama, Louisiana, Mississippi, and South Carolina, receiving more than a million votes. He heralded this opinion:

"Segregation in the South is honest, open and above-board. Of the two systems, or styles of segregation, the Northern and the Southern, there is no doubt whatever in my mind which is the better."

By the 1990s Republicans were starting to win more elections in the South, due in part to evangelical Christians siding with that party and Democrats not appealing to them.

* * *

When Democrats kind of cavalierly attack the religious right or go after Pat Robertson or Jerry Falwell, our candidates have sent the signal to a lot of religious people, "Well, I guess they are not interested in me." And I think this includes a lot of people who would fit very naturally within the Democratic Party.

      —Tim Kaine, US senator from Virginia

I have people ask me if I'm going to convince my daughters to be Democrats, and I say, "I have yet to convince my daughters to close a door." I don't know how in the world I would ever convince them to be in a political affiliation.

      —James Carville, political commentator
        and media personality

Worst damn fool mistake I ever made was letting myself be elected Vice President of the United States. Should have stuck with my old chores as Speaker of the House. I gave up the second most important job in the government for one that didn't amount to a hill of beans. I spent eight long years as Mr. Roosevelt's spare tire.

—John Nance Garner, thirty-second
vice president of the United States

Republicans are the party of "no," and Democrats are the party of "don't know," because it hasn't fought for bold ideas, policies, or plans to turn us in a new direction.

—Jesse Jackson, activist

The job of elected officials is to answer to the people who sent them to Washington—not to scorn them, not to demean them, not to mock them, and not to sell their jobs and dreams to the highest bidder.

—Jeff Sessions, former US attorney general

A lot of celebrities relish politics and are eager to lend their names to candidates and causes. I never wanted to be a spokesman for anybody.
—Charley Pride, singer

Barney spotted our neighbor's lawn, where he promptly took care of his business. There I was, the former president of the United States, with a plastic bag on my hand, picking up that which I had been dodging for the past eight years.

—George W. Bush, forty-third president of the United States, *Decision Points*

Since almost all Negroes are workers, live on wages, and suffer from the high cost of food, clothing and shelter, it is obvious that the Republican and Democratic Parties are opposed to their interests.

—Asa Philip Randolph, activist

One of these days, someone smarter and younger and more articulate than I is going to get through to the American people just how really messed up the federal government has become. And when that happens, the American people are going to rise up like that football crowd in Cleveland and run both teams off the field.

—Zell Miller, former governor of Georgia and US senator

Being president is like being a jackass
in a hailstorm. There's nothing to do
but to stand there and take it.
—Lyndon B. Johnson, thirty-sixth
president of the United States

It's innate in me to be a Democrat—a true Southern populist
kind of Democrat. There's not a lot of those anymore. I'm
not saying I'm right or wrong. That's just the way I feel.

—Tim McGraw, singer

For some reason, a lot of folks seem to think that until
very recently every Southern politician would go home at
night, wait for it to get dark, take a white sheet out of his
closet, and then go tearing around the countryside, burning
crosses and raising hell.

—Herman E. Talmadge, author,
Talmadge: A Political Legacy,
A Politician's Life: A Memoir

A Republican in my state of Arkansas feels about as out of place as Michael Vick at the Westminster dog show.
　　　　　—Mike Huckabee, former governor of Arkansas

The more you observe politics, the more you've got to admit that each party is worse than the other.
　　　　　　—Will Rogers, humorist and actor

A national political campaign is better than the best circus ever heard of, with a mass baptism and a couple of hangings thrown in.
　　　　　　—H. L. Mencken, journalist

I hold that establishing mixed schools will not harm the white race. I am their friend. I said in Mississippi, and I say here, and I say everywhere, that I would abandon the Republican Party if it went into any measures of legislation really damaging to any portion of the white race, but it is not in the Republican Party to do that.
　　　　　—Hiram Rhodes Revels, former US senator from Mississippi, and the first African-American senator

Give a member of Congress a junket and a mimeograph machine and he thinks he is secretary of state.
—Dean Rusk, fifty-fourth US secretary of state

Washington, DC, is a city filled with people who believe they are important.
—David Brinkley, journalist

I'm very liberal in some ways, and then I'm very conservative in others. I once asked my grandpa, "Are you a Republican or a Democrat?" He said, "I'm a Democrat, but I'm saving up to be a Republican."
—Kenny Chesney, singer

I would rather be beaten, and be a man, than to be elected and be a little puppy dog.
—Davy Crockett, frontiersman and US congressman from Tennessee

I was asked for years about being a Republican, probably because most black people are Democrats. My mother heard it once and called me and said, "Charles, Republicans are for the rich people." And I said, "Mom, I'm rich."
— Charles Barkley, former professional basketball player and sports commentator, *I May Be Wrong But I Doubt It*

I believe being a good senator requires two things. Number one, acumen. Number two, interest.

—Trey Gowdy, US senator from South Carolina

Cotton on the roadside, cotton in the ditch
We all picked the cotton but we never got rich
Daddy was a veteran, a Southern Democrat
They oughta get a rich man to vote like that.

—Alabama, "Song of the South"

You all got only three friends in this world: the Lord God Almighty, the Sears Roebuck catalog, and Eugene Talmadge. And you can only vote for one of them.

—Eugene Talmadge, former US senator from Georgia

I don't have any faith in the Republican Party. I don't have any faith in the Democrat Party. The only hope for this nation is God.

—Franklin Graham, evangelist

What's going on in the Senate is kind of a politics of escalation. We're getting sort of like the Mideast: pay back everybody when you're in charge.

—Lindsey Graham, US senator from South Carolina

I come from the South and I know what war is, for I have seen its terrible wreckage and ruin. It is easy for me as President to declare war. I do not have to fight, and neither do the gentlemen on the Hill who now clamor for it. It is some poor farmer's boy, or the son of some poor widow, who will have to do the fighting and dying.

—Woodrow Wilson, twenty-eighth president of the United States

It is time to move away from advise and obstruct and get back to advise and consent.

—Mitch McConnell, US senator from Kentucky

My father joined our party because the Democrats in Jim Crow Alabama of 1952 would not register him to vote. The Republicans did.

—Condoleezza Rice, sixty-sixth US secretary of state

The preservation of the sacred fire of liberty and the destiny of the republican model of government are justly considered . . . deeply . . . finally, staked on the experiment entrusted to the hands of the American people.

—George Washington, first president of the United States

CHAPTER 10

Observations from Visitors

Chances are, people tell more jokes about the South than any other region in the United States, or the world. As a rule, a Southerner has a good sense of humor and might tell a funny story himself, but it's another thing hearing one from an outsider.

Additionally, terms such as *redneck*, *hillbilly*, *hick*, and *white trash* are all derogatory descriptions of people who live in the South, or those who are originally from the region. Southerners often are collectively seen as racists, for example, when a person who happens to be from the South and is a white supremacist is interviewed by the media.

Think about books, movies, or TV programs depicting life in the South. For some reason, Southerners have the reputation of being caught up in the past and never recovering from the Civil War. As a result, Southerners are considered backward and discriminatory. The movie *Sweet Home Alabama* includes a Civil War reenactment scene, and TV's *The Beverly Hillbillies* series was a big hit for several years with scenes such as the Jethro Bodine character bragging about finally graduating from the sixth grade when he was in his thirties.

Others poke fun at Southern accents and assume that because a person speaks with a drawl and uses Southernized words (such as "Coke" for a soft drink, or "buggy" for a grocery cart), a Southerner is not as intelligent as those from other regions.

On the other hand, those not from the South often romanticize the area and picture all Southerners as genteel souls with oak-lined drives leading up to their plantation-style homes. Other people's observations can be good and bad, but usually are inaccurate.

*　*　*

I think of myself as a Hollywood hillbilly, but I'm sick of all these questions people ask about Alabama. "Do you have an outhouse?" "Is there a lot of inbreeding in your family?" They think all Southerners don't have computers and TV sets and that we're all still living in 1862.

　　　　　　　　　　　　　　　　—Sunny Mabrey, actress

People don't go, "I'm a proud Floridian." They just don't. It's like nobody owns the state, and there are people just constantly showing up in the state for various reasons. I would say we're like the Ellis Island for stupid, weird people. If you want to pleasure yourself into a stuffed animal in a Walmart, you're going to go to Florida to do that. You want to get naked by the side of the road for no apparent reason, Florida's the place you would like, if nothing else, because it's warmer there.

—Dave Barry, humorist and writer, *Conversations with Tyler*

Every culture has its southerners—people who work
as little as they can, preferring to dance, drink, sing,
brawl, kill their unfaithful spouses; who have livelier
gestures, more lustrous eyes, more colorful garments,
more fancifully decorated vehicles, a wonderful sense of
rhythm, and charm, charm, charm; unambitious, no, lazy,
ignorant, superstitious, uninhibited people, never on time,
conspicuously poorer (how could it be otherwise, say the
northerners); who for all their poverty and squalor lead
enviable lives—envied, that is, by work-driven, sensually
inhibited, less corruptly governed northerners. We are
superior to them, say the northerners, clearly superior.
    —Susan Sontag, author, *The Volcano Lover: A Romance*

We got out of the car for air and suddenly
both of us were stoned with joy to realize that
in the darkness all around us was fragrant
green grass and the smell of fresh manure
and warm waters. "We're in the South!
We've left the winter!" Faint daybreak
illuminated green shoots by the side of the
road. I took a deep breath; a locomotive
howled across the darkness, mobile-bound.
So were we. I took off my shirt and exulted.
    —Jack Kerouac, author, *On the Road*

It gets so hot in the South, the hardware stores sell thermometers with readings of Fahrenheit, Celsius, and Holy Crap.

—Glenn Frey, musician

We won the war because we had a righteous cause and better songs. "Mine eyes have seen the glory of the coming of the Lord" vs. "I wish I was in the land of cotton, old times there are not forgotten"—there's no comparison. Ours has watchfires in it, flaring lamps, a trumpet, jubilant feet. The old times in the land of cotton were not enjoyed by the people who picked the cotton, but by the ones who sat on the porch with their mint juleps and wrote bad poetry about sunsets and weeping willows.

—Garrison Keillor, *Washington Post*, January 12, 2017

I've just come back from Mississippi, and over there, when you talk about the West Bank, they think you mean Arkansas.

—Pat Buchanan, politician

Collecting statistics at Camp Zachary Taylor after the Armistice [World War I, 1918], I found that out of two hundred and fifty men from Kentucky and Tennessee, ninety were completely illiterate, several were actual imbeciles, two had syphilitic rheumatism, and any number had married at childhood ages, from twelve–the youngest– to seventeen. They had married girls from nine–the youngest–to fourteen. So I am ready to believe that the Faulkner and Caldwell depictions of ingrown sections of the country are based upon actual conditions.

–Kay Boyle, author, *Being Geniuses Together, 1920–1930*

One time at the University of Colorado, at a faculty dinner, this professor said to me, "Well, my goodness, a boy from Appa-lay-chee-a with a PhD!" The dinner was in her house. And I said, "My grandparents didn't have indoor plumbing, but they had more books in their house than you do." I was a little insulted by the Appa-lay-chee-a business.

–Charles Frazier, writer

There is a growing feeling that perhaps Texas is really another country, a place where the skies, the disasters, the diamonds, the politicians, the women, the fortunes, the football players and the murders are all bigger than anywhere else.

–Pete Hamill, writer

139

There's also way too much religion in the South to be consistent with good mental health. Still, I love traveling down there, especially when I'm in the mood for a quick trip to the thirteenth century. I'm not someone who buys into all that "New South" shit you hear; I judge a place by the number of lynchings they've had, overall.

–George Carlin, comedian

Southern Appalachians have been ridiculed since the country began. In fiction, they're usually depicted in a cartoonish manner. The region is poor, and very suspicious of outsiders, so there's a sort of "us versus them" situation. They're easy to poke fun at.

–Barbara Kingsolver, author

The most beautiful voice in the word is that of an educated Southern woman.

–Winston Churchill, former prime minister of Britain

I never ceased to be surprised when Southern whites, at their homes or clubs, told racial jokes and spoke so derogatorily of blacks while longtime servants, for whom they quite clearly had some affection, were well within earshot.

–Walter Cronkite, journalist

Kentucky woman
If she get to know you
She goin' to own you
Kentucky woman.
—Neil Diamond, singer, "Kentucky Woman"

Texas women have an amazing sense of purpose when they lose it. They're the best girls in the world—they're loyal and fun, but when they get mad, they'll try to kill you.
—John Cusack, actor

I remember, when I went away to college at Southern Methodist University in Dallas, my aunt sent me a book with the rules of being a Southern Belle. One of the rules was to never wear white after Labor Day. Fashion has a lot to do with confidence and making up your own rules.
—Kourtney Kardashian, reality TV star

To the best of my judgment, I have labored for, and not against, the Union. As I have not felt, so I have not expressed any harsh sentiment towards our Southern brethren. I have constantly declared, as I really believed, the only difference between them and us is the difference of circumstances.
—Abraham Lincoln, sixteenth president of the United States

When I chose to leave a career as a young lawyer in Washington to move to Arkansas to marry Bill and start a family, my friends asked, "Are you out of your mind?"
—Hillary Clinton, former first lady of the United States and sixty-seventh US secretary of state

There's something about Southern women that is so unique, yet so universal. Strong Southern women are allowed to be soft and feminine and have a sense of humor. But what I love about Southern women in particular is their universality.

—Connie Britton, actress

We could say that people who eat grits, listen to country music, follow stock-car racing, support corporal punishment in the schools, hunt 'possum, go to Baptist churches and prefer bourbon to Scotch are likely to be Southerners.

—John Shelton Reed, sociologist and author

It was always so hot, and everyone was so polite, and everything was all surface, but underneath it was like a bomb waiting to go off. I always felt that way about the South, that beneath the smiles and Southern hospitality and politeness were a lot of guns and liquor and secrets.

—James McBride, author, *The Color of Water: A Black Man's Tribute to His White Mother*

The prevalence of mobile homes does not correspond with the prevalence of poverty, or with much of anything else. All that can be confidently said about America's mobile homes is that they are massed in places where you wouldn't want to be in one. Florida's mobile homes lie athwart the path of hurricanes. Georgia's are in the way of tornadoes.

—P. J. O'Rourke, writer

There's a Southern accent, where I come from
The young 'uns call it country, the Yankees call it dumb
I got my own way of talking, but everything gets done
With a Southern accent, where I come from.

—Tom Petty, "Southern Accents"

The American high school graduate is two years behind his English, French or German counterpart; in Alabama, God knows how far behind.

—Gore Vidal, writer

He had met this sort of white man before, earnest and believing what came out of their mouths. The veracity of their words was another matter, but at least they believed them. The Southern white man was spat from the loins of the devil and there was no way to forecast his next evil act.

—Colson Whitehead, author, *The Underground Railroad*

CHAPTER 11

Relationships and Family

Generally speaking, most Southerners are good friends and remarkably close to their immediate and extended families. They adore their mamas and daddies, and usually don't stray too far from home even after they've married and started families of their own. If they do move away, they'll most likely come back home eventually. They learn good manners and social niceties from their parents, who were taught the ways of Southern life by their mamas and daddies before them.

For the most part, Southerners also are affectionate souls who hug and kiss friends every time they're together and say "I love you" before they walk out the screened door. That's another thing about Southerners. Through the years they have come up with what seems like their own dictionary of endearments, like these: sweetheart, baby, sugar, darlin,' dumplin,' honeybunch—and the list goes on and on. Oh yeah, nicknames, too, such as doodlebug, junior, and buck. Hear one of those names before meeting the person, and you can bet the family farm that he's from down south.

Writer Tim Heaton recalled how he was given his nickname: "The most persistent nicknames are the names given to us by family. In my case, I could not pronounce 'Tim' when I was little. Instead, I said, 'Tee-Tee.' My grandparents called me Tee-Tee all their lives. Eventually, this was shortened to 'Tee' by my parents and sister. It was also a good nickname for a kid who played golf. My dad would often call me 'Tiger Tee' if I did well in school or athletics—it makes me smile to this day when I think of it."

* * *

To the newcomer to the South, hearing that a coworker plans a weekend visit to "mama and them's" (the correct plural possessive, don'tcha know) might make him think that mama has been left alone either through an act of scoundreldom involving the town's resident hoochie-mama (an altogether different kind of mama) or Daddy's untimely demise.

—Celia Rivenbark, writer

I came up poor. My mother only had a fourth-grade education. My dad didn't have any education at all. But they were very structured. They worked hard. You know, they didn't complain. They didn't murmur. And they believe in the Christ.

—Evander Holyfield, professional boxer

We are the people our parents warned us about.

—Jimmy Buffett, singer-songwriter

You always want to break away from your parents, and you always think, "I'm never going to be like that guy." What I've discovered is you kind of wind up becoming your parents, which is also a cliché in itself. My father, despite the fact that he's been dead for over twenty-five years, he's been a huge influence on me.

—Loudon Wainwright III, musician

I have found it easier to identify with the characters who verge upon hysteria, who were frightened of life, who were desperate to reach out to another person. But these seemingly fragile people are the strong people really.

—Tennessee Williams, playwright

Bubba was my best good friend. And even I know that ain't somethin' you can find just around the corner.

—Tom Hanks as Forrest, *Forrest Gump*

I grew up in the South. I grew up reading novels, not newspapers. And I grew up in a family of ten people. All of these to me are the formative elements of how I approach the world and how I approach stories. Journalism has always been at its base for me about stories, and I think that has something to do with having grown up in the South, which is a story culture.

—Mary Schmich, columnist for the *Chicago Tribune*

All my life I had to fight. I had to fight my daddy. I had to fight my brothers. I had to fight my cousins and my uncles. A girl child ain't safe in a family of men. But I never thought I'd have to fight in my own house. She let out her breath. I loves Harpo, she say. God knows I do. But I'll kill him dead before I let him beat me.
—Alice Walker, author, *The Color Purple*

Hoke, you're my best friend."
—Jessica Tandy as Daisy Werthan, *Driving Miss Daisy*

Stop using the word *bromance*. Can we please kill that stupid term? We're just friends. It's called friendship!
—Blake Shelton, singer

I don't believe professional athletes should be role models. I believe parents should be role models . . . It's not like it was when I was growing up. My mom and my grandmother told me how it was going to be. If I didn't like it, they said, Don't let the door hit you in the ass on your way out. Parents have to take better control.
—Charles Barkley, former professional basketball player and sports commentator

My whole family are hams. They're storytellers and everyone outdoes the next one.

—Matthew McConaughey, actor

My mother thought Hollywood was a den of iniquity, and people came to terrible bad ends there.

—Kitty Carlisle, actress

I'm a true country Southern girl that has always been built around family, cookouts and gatherings and being together on the holidays, singing together and laughing together. So whenever God opened doors for me to be able to travel the world and sing and do all the great things that I've done, I didn't want to lose that part, so family first for me.

—Fantasia Barrino, singer

Every man sees in his relatives, and especially in his cousins, a series of grotesque caricatures of himself.

—H. L. Mencken, journalist

You have to understand, now, I'm a momma's boy. I'm from the South. My way of being raised is totally different than the big city life. I truly was a country boy.

—Terry Bradshaw, former quarterback for the Pittsburgh Steelers and TV sports commentator

I was raised by a lady that was crippled all her life but she did everything for me and she raised me. She washed our clothes, cooked our food, she did everything for us. I don't think I ever heard her complain a day in her life. She taught me responsibility towards my brother and sisters and the community.

—Ernest Gaines, writer

I learned to read a little in my primer, to write my own name, and to cypher some in the three first rules in figures. And this was all the schooling I ever had in my life, up to this day. I should have continued longer if it hadn't been that I concluded I couldn't do any longer without a wife, and so I cut out to hunt me one.

—Davy Crockett, frontiersman and congressman from Tennessee

I'm sure there were times when I wish I had thought, "Gosh, that might really embarrass Mom and Dad," but our parents didn't raise us to think about them. They're very selfless and they wanted us to have as normal of a college life as possible. So really, we didn't think of any repercussions.

—Jenna Bush Hager, television personality

Listen, I come from the most screwed-up, dysfunctional situation. You've got violence. Police at your house. Your dad's gone. Nowhere to live. I want people to know, if I can make it, anybody can make it.

—Dabo Swinney, football coach for Clemson University

The best money advice ever given me was from my father. When I was a little girl, he told me, "Don't spend anything unless you have to."

—Dinah Shore, singer/actress

I don't want to be mushy about it, but having four kids is definitely the best thing that has ever happened to me, and each kid is, to me, more fascinating than any five movies.

—Warren Beatty, actor

My mother is a ball of fire in the world, and I love that about her. But what I have learned from my stepdad is something as important, which is patience and compassion. Because when you are living with someone else, those two qualities go a long way.

—Justin Timberlake, singer

My mother read secondarily for information; she sank as a hedonist into novels. She read Dickens in the spirit in which she would have eloped with him.

—Eudora Welty, author, *One Writer's Beginnings*

I think my dad is a lot cooler than other dads. He still acts like he's still seventeen.

—Miley Cyrus, singer/actress

My grandmother started walking five miles a day when she was sixty. She's ninety-seven now, and we don't know where the hell she is.

—Ellen DeGeneres, comedian

If you ever start feeling like you have the goofiest, craziest, most dysfunctional family in the world, all you have to do is go to a state fair. Because five minutes at the fair, you'll be going, "You know, we're all right. We are dang near royalty."

—Jeff Foxworthy, humorist and author

There ain't nobody I'd rather have alongside me in a fight than my mama with a broken bottle in her hand.
—Hank Williams, musician

If same-sex relationships are really sinful, then why do they so often produce good fruit—loving families, open homes, self-sacrifice, commitment, faithfulness, joy? And if conservative Christians are really right in their response to same-sex relationships, then why does that response often produce bad fruit—secrets, shame, depression, loneliness, broken families, and fear?
—Rachel Held Evans, author and blogger

I was an adopted child of my grandparents, and I don't know how I can ever express my gratitude for that, because my parents would have been a mess, you know.
—James Earl Jones, actor

It's quite a thing, if you've never been in or known a small Southern town. The people are not particularly sophisticated, naturally. They're not worldly wise in any way. But they tell you a story whenever they see you.
—Harper Lee, author

I think I've got my business notions and my sense for that sort of thing from my dad. My dad never had a chance to go to school. He couldn't read and write. But he was so smart. He was just one of those people that could just make the most of anything and everything that he had to work with.

—Dolly Parton, singer

Before I was married to Martin and became a King, I was a proud Scott, shaped by my mother's discernment and my father's strength.

—Coretta Scott King, activist

My mom used to make everything. She had a great garden and composted and made everything from scratch—peanut butter, bread, jelly, everything. I don't know how she did it because all those things take time and love and labor. I only do half the stuff she does—but there's still time.

—Julia Roberts, actress

In large measure, black Southern writers owe their clarity of vision to parents who refused to diminish themselves as human beings by succumbing to racism. Our parents seemed to know that an extreme negative emotion held against other human beings for reasons they do not control can be blinding. Blindness about other human beings, especially for a writer, is equivalent to death.

—Alice Walker, author,
The Black Writer and the Southern Experience

Once a bitch always a bitch, what I say.

—William Faulkner, author, *The Sound and the Fury*

I grew up in a small town in West Virginia, and most of my family lived in our neighborhood or very close by. I had my grandparents down the street, my great-grandmother next door, and my great-aunt and great-uncle one door down.

—Katie Lee, chef

Mama had an appreciation of the language. She taught me a love of words, of how they should be used and how they can fill a creative soul with a passion and lead to a life's work.
—Lewis Grizzard, humorist and writer,
Don't Forget to Call Your Mama . . .
I Wish I Could Call Mine

Growing up, I started developing confidence in what I felt. My parents helped me to believe in myself. I wasn't the best-looking guy, I wasn't the best athlete in the world, but they made me feel good about myself.
—Herschel Walker,
former professional football player

Madea is a Southern term. It's short for "Mother dear." So there are a lot of Madeas out there.
—Tyler Perry, actor

I finished high school, moved to Nashville for college, and set out to break into the music business. Every night when I called home with news of my experiences, my mom and dad would encourage me to keep taking those small steps.
—Trisha Yearwood, singer

During my last days at Florida State, 65 to 70 percent of my boys did not have a daddy at home. They're raised by mommas. Thank God for them mommas, or grandmommas. Or big sister or aunt.

—Bobby Bowden, former football coach for Florida State University

A man blessed with a good mamma and a good wife has no right to complain about anything else.
—Claude Pepper, former US senator from Florida

The earliest memories I have of my mother must have been when I was around five. One was baking cakes, which she loved to do. I can see them now ready in the pantry for Christmas; there was fruit cake, both the dark and the light, for which the citron and raisins, currants and spices, had been set out in little piles; there were rosie cake, tinted with cochineal; marble cake, with streaking of chocolate and white; spice cake, angel cake; coconut cake; sponge cake; pound cake, and others; one Christmas there were seventeen of them.

—Stark Young, author

My parents were not affluent people and were not—didn't come from the extremities of education. My mother had a high school diploma. I often think I so wish she'd come out of the hills in Appalachia and been able to go on to college. I think she would have made a wonderful teacher.
—Dwight Yoakam, singer, on *The Tavis Smiley Show*

I learned a lot from the stories my uncle, aunts and grandparents told me: that no one is perfect but most people are good; that people can't be judged by their worst or weakest moments; that harsh judgments can make hypocrites of us all; that a lot of life is just showing up and hanging on; that laughter is often the best, and sometimes the only, response to pain.
—Bill Clinton, former US president and author, *My Life*

My sister took me as her own. My mum had a lot of help raising me. That's what happens in large families: your siblings raise you.

—Holly Hunter, actress

My parents are proud of their Indian heritage, but they came halfway across the world so their children could be born here, raised here as Americans. They came legally, but they came here in search of the American dream, in search of freedom and opportunity.

—Bobby Jindal, former governor of Louisiana

CHAPTER 12

Love, Romance, and Lust, By Golly

Southerners tend to wear their hearts on their sleeves and tell it like it is, even when it comes to their innermost thoughts about love, romance, and lust. Who could forget when Jimmy Carter was running for president and had this shocking admission in an interview in *Playboy* magazine? "I've looked on many women with lust. I've committed adultery in my heart many times. God knows I will do this and forgives me."

When the magazine hit the newsstands, Americans were stunned that Carter would admit to such feelings. But that's the way Southerners are: frank, candid, and quite innocent when it comes to speaking their minds.

Country music lyrics as well as beach music songs, both of which originated in the South, can be suggestive and full of love, lust, and romance all at once. Country singer Conway Twitty had a hit record with "I'd Love to Lay You Down."

There's a lot of ways of saying what I want to say to you
There's songs and poems and promises
and dreams that might come true
But I won't talk of starry skies or moonlight on the ground
I'll come right out and tell you I'd just love to lay you down.
Lay you down and softly whisper
pretty love words in your ear
Lay you down and tell you all the
things a woman loves to hear
I'll let you know how much it means just having you around
Oh darlin', how I'd love to lay you down . . .

Plenty of Southerners of a certain generation have danced the shag to suggestive beach music songs with titillating titles such as "39-21-46," "Give Me Just a Little More Time," and "You're More than a Number in My Little Red Book."

Consider these lyrics to "Double Shot (of My Baby's Love)" by the Swingin' Medallions:

> Woke up this morning, my head was so bad
> The worst hangover that I ever had
> What happened to me last night
> That girl of mine, she loved me so right (yeah) (oh, oh)
> She loved me so long and she loved me so hard
> I finally passed out in her front yard (whoo)
> It wasn't wine that I had too much of
> It was a double shot of my baby's love.

Those words are enough to make a girl blush.

* * *

"She was a big ol' ho," Riley told her brother. "She put out more than the Tab machine in the Tri-Delta house."
—Mary Kay Andrews, author, *The Weekenders*

I do like men and I had, you know, a guy in high school that I wanted to marry desperately. He's the mayor of some small town in Texas. I could be the mayor's wife right now.
—Ellen DeGeneres, comedian

I'm sick of the whole thing, too. You try to bring two people together and what do you get? Heartaches!
—Don Knotts as Barney Fife, *The Andy Griffith Show*

I have learned that only two things are necessary to keep one's wife happy. First, let her think she's having her own way. And second, let her have it.
—Lyndon B. Johnson, thirty-sixth president of the United States

She is pale but affectionate, clinging to his arm—always clinging to his arm. Anyone can see that she is a peach and of the cling variety.
—O. Henry, author, "A Tempered Wind"

I thought I told you to wait in the car.
—Tallulah Bankhead, actress, on seeing a former lover for the first time in years

Storytelling and copulation are the two chief forms of amusement in the South. They're inexpensive and easy to procure.
—Robert Penn Warren, writer

I've been married five times, and people think that's some bizarre thing, yet I've got buddies who refuse to get married and have sex with fifteen people a week. I'm like, "Which is better?" At least I was trying.

Billy Bob Thornton, actor

There'll be fifteen minutes of kissing
Then you'll holler "Please don't stop" (Don't stop!)
There'll be fifteen minutes of teasing
And fifteen minutes of squeezing
And fifteen minutes of blowing my top.
—Billy Ward and His Dominoes, "Sixty Minute Man"

Grown men should not be having sex with prostitutes unless they are married to them.

—Jerry Falwell, late televangelist and leader of the Moral Majority

I think what makes our marriage work amid all the glare is that my husband is my best friend. He inspires everything in my life and enables me to do the best that I can. I want to hang out with him more than anyone.

—Faith Hill, singer, about her husband, Tim McGraw

Love is the main generator of all good writing . . . Love, passion, compassion, are all welded together.
—Carson McCullers, writer

Love is an ice cream sundae, with all the marvelous coverings. Sex is the cherry on top.
—Jimmy Dean, singer

All you need for happiness is a good gun, a good horse, and a good wife.
—Daniel Boone, frontiersman

A woman has got to love a bad man once or twice in her life, to be thankful for a good one.
—Marjorie Kinnan Rawlings, author, *The Yearling*

She's a devil, she's an angel,
she's a woman, she's a child.
She's a heartache when she leaves you,
But she'll leave you with a smile.
—George Strait, "She'll Leave You with a Smile"

"No, I don't think I will kiss you, although you need kissing, badly. That's what's wrong with you. You should be kissed, and often, and by someone who knows how."
  —Rhett Butler to Scarlett O'Hara in *Gone with the Wind*

When we got married—almost ten years ago now—we made a commitment to really be together, which means we hardly ever spend a night apart. And being madly in love is important, but I think it's equally important to be in deep like! I like this guy . . . we talk about everything, and we laugh a lot. Life is good!

—Trisha Yearwood, singer, about her
marriage to Garth Brooks

My parents have always been vocal about "the birds and the bees." People who watched the *Duck Dynasty* episode in which my dad gave Willie's son John Luke and his girlfriend the sex talk while motoring down the river in a boat might not be surprised that I heard this exact speech countless times in my childhood. I remember coming home one day after hearing my buddies talking about sexually transmitted diseases and asking my dad about it. I don't remember the specifics of his speech, but I would never forget the last thing he said. "Son, you keep that thing in your pocket until you get married and you'll never have to worry about it," he told me.

—Jase Robertson, author,
Good Call: Reflections on Faith, Family, and Fowl

Who are your friends? They are the people who are there in hard times or when you're hurting beyond words. Or with a few words of encouragement and concern, make you realize you're really not lost at all. Friends comes in both sexes, in all shapes, colors and sizes, but the most important thing they have in common is the ability to share with you, your best joys and your deepest sorrows, for they are your friends.
—Glen Campbell, author, *Rhinestone Cowboy*

Ladies have come up with all these expressions to reassure men. "Oh, honey, it's not the size of the ship, it's the motion of the ocean." That may be true, but it takes a long time to get to England in a rowboat.

—Jeff Foxworthy, humorist and author

He's just like my father that way—my father just adored my mother and let her do whatever she wanted. John's like that. He's a very rare man, a very good man, and I've had a good life with him. I'm proud to be walking in the wake of Johnny's fame.

—June Carter Cash, singer, about her husband, Johnny Cash

Well, I courted her as proper as proper can be.
First off I wrote her a love note asking
her to go on out with me.
And then I tied it on to the prettiest rock ya ever did see.
And then I give it the prettiest toss ya ever did
see . . . right through the front window!

—Howard Morris as Ernest T. Bass, *The Andy Griffith Show*

We're all a little weird. And life is a little weird. And when
we find someone whose weirdness is compatible with
ours, we join up with them and fall into mutually satisfying
weirdness—and call it love—true love.

—Robert Fulghum, author, *True Love*

It is really rare to find someone you really, really love and
that you want to spend your life with and all that stuff that
goes along with being married. I am one of those lucky
people. And I think she feels that way too. So the romantic
stuff is easy because you want them to be happy.

—Harry Connick Jr., singer

Yes, the companionship is amazing. You know, you can
get that physical attraction that happens is great, but then
there's an awful lot of time and the rest of the day that you
have to fill.

—Vince Gill, singer, who is married to Amy Grant

I know this is kind of corny, but we thought
about renewing our vows again because I
think my mom would really love it if we did
that in Arkansas, where I came from.
—Mary Steenburgen, actress, who
is married to Ted Danson

True love, to me, is when she's the first thought that goes through your head when you wake up and the last thought that goes through your head before you go to sleep.

—Justin Timberlake, singer

All I knew growing up was that my father was married to and loved my momma, period. He worked hard, made some money, and put it on the dresser. She spent it on the family, and he went out and earned some more. He taught me the most about love.

—Steve Harvey, game-show host

The word *romance*, according to the dictionary, means excitement, adventure, and something extremely real. Romance should last a lifetime.

—Billy Graham, late evangelist

In the South there's a difference between "naked" and "nekkid." "Naked" means you don't have any clothes on. "Nekkid" means you don't have any clothes on and you're up to something.

—Lewis Grizzard, humorist, author, and newspaper columnist

171

And he don't know . . .
that I dug my key into the side of his pretty
little souped-up four-wheel drive,
carved my name into his leather seats.
I took a Louisville slugger to both headlights,
slashed a hole in all four tires . . .
Maybe next time he'll think before he cheats.
                    —Carrie Underwood, "Before He Cheats"

Hard work is damn near as overrated as monogamy.
                    —Huey Long, former governor of Louisiana

And when we get behind closed doors
Then she lets her hair hang down
And she makes me glad that I'm a man
Oh, no one knows what goes on behind closed doors.
                    —Charlie Rich, "Behind Closed Doors"

We went skinny-dipping and we did things that frightened
the fish.
                    —Julia Roberts as Shelby, *Steel Magnolias*

[W]hen you put on your shortest dress, please leave some mystery in it. That's the difference between a miniskirt and a ho-skirt. A ho-skirt shows your Frisbee. A miniskirt shows just enough to cause some mystery. What these young women lack is mystery.

—Tyler Perry, *Don't Make a Black Woman Take Off Her Earrings: Madea's Uninhibited Commentaries on Love and Life*

You have to understand that women in the South, women of Southern blood, just don't partake in scandalous adventures, and when we do, it's in a discreet manner. We have reputations to consider, after all.

—Blake O'Hara Heart, author, *The Sassy Belles*

I had someone correct my grammar once on a blind date, and within the first ten minutes the date was over. You just don't correct somebody's grammar. That's just not okay. I'm from Tennessee, so I probably say everything wrong. I might have said ain't, or something like that.

—Reese Witherspoon, actress and producer

I'm not trying to be sexy. It's just my way of expressing myself when I move around.

—Elvis Presley, singer

The point is that getting married for lust or money or social status or even love is usually trouble. The point is that marriage is a maze into which we wander—a maze that is best got through with a great companion.

—Robert Fulghum, author, *It Was On Fire When I Lay Down On It*

Sexiness wears thin after a while and beauty fades, but to be married to a man who makes you laugh every day, ah, now that's a real treat.

—Joanne Woodward, actress

Stand by your man
Give him two arms to cling to
And something warm to come to
When nights are cold and lonely.

—Tammy Wynette, "Stand By Your Man"

CHAPTER 13

On Life, Death, and a Bit of Homegrown Advice

Any Southerner worth his salt—or weight in gold, for that matter—can carry on a conversation with a perfect stranger and end up talking about life and death. Offering unsolicited advice or giving out too much information are both characteristic of honest-to-goodness Southerners.

When it comes to a death in the South, be prepared for a long, drawn-out celebration of life. Funeral rituals in the South often drag on for days at a time, culminating with the visitation, service, burial, and luncheon afterwards. Those who pay their respects at the visitation might overhear others discussing the departed with the family. They mean well, with comments like these: "She looks so natural," "She's finally at peace," and "Thank the Lord her suffering is over." Others may cup their hands to their mouths and whisper to one another: "She looks a hundred times better than she did at the hospital," or "Why on earth did they put that picture of her ex-husband in the coffin with her?"

Mourners may even sprinkle around a few adages that combine sayings about life and death, such as: "Life goes on," "That's life," or "Death is a part of life."

Then there's always the advice that a Southerner can dish out not just at funeral visitations but anytime. People from the South are forever telling it like they think it is, and why others should think their way.

* * *

It's life. You don't figure it out. You just climb up on the beast and ride.

—Rebecca Wells, author, *Divine Secrets of the Ya-Ya Sisterhood*

You've got to continue to grow, or you're just like last night's cornbread—stale and dry.

—Loretta Lynn, author, *Loretta Lynn: Coal Miner's Daughter*

To succeed in life, you need three things: a wishbone, a backbone and a funny bone.
—Reba McIntire, singer

There was clearly nothing to do but flop down on the shabby little couch and howl. So Della did it. Which instigates the moral reflection that life is made up of sobs, sniffles, and smiles, with sniffles predominating.

—O. Henry, author, *The Gift of the Magi*

A purpose gives meaning to life. It is like the hub in a wheel–with every spoke fitted into it to make a strong and perfect circle. Without such a hub, spokes will not radiate evenly and your wheel will lack strength, will tend to break apart on the first good bump it hits. Given a strong hub, a strong purpose, a person can take a surprising number of shocks and bumps on the outside rim without sustaining permanent damage.

–Oveta Culp Hobby, first secretary of the US Department of Health, Education and Welfare

Life is a moderately good play with a badly written third act.

–Truman Capote, writer

All your life, you will be faced with a choice. You can choose love, positivity, and gratitude that things aren't worse, or hate, negativity, and bitterness that things aren't better . . . I choose love, positivity, and gratitude that things aren't worse.

–Johnny Cash, singer

Learning how to be still, to really be still and let life happen–that stillness becomes a radiance.

–Morgan Freeman, actor

Pretend that every single person you meet has a sign around his or her neck that says, "Make me feel important." Not only will you succeed in sales, you will succeed in life.

—Mary Kay Ash, founder of Mary Kay Cosmetics

Find something in life that you love doing. If you make a lot of money, that's a bonus, and if you don't, you still won't hate going to work.

—Jeff Foxworthy, humorist and author

You can get all A's and still flunk life.

—Walker Percy, writer

Older and wiser voices can help you find the right path, if you are only willing to listen.

—Jimmy Buffett, singer

I don't feel that no big stone should be put over my head, saying he did this, he did that. Unless there's something that I really did do. I believe I'm just ordinary. And I'd like for people to think of me that way, as just a guy that tried. Wanted to be loved by other people because he loved people.

—B. B. King, musician

There ain't nothin' to dyin', really. You just get tired. You kind of drift away.

—James Dickey, author

I sometimes wonder how many of these lifetime achievement awards you can accept before you have to do the decent thing and die.

—James Taylor, singer

I couldn't have foreseen all the good things that have followed my mother's death. The renewed energy, the surprising sweetness of grief. The tenderness I feel for strangers on walkers. The deeper love I have for my siblings and friends. The desire to play the mandolin. The gift of a visitation.

—Mary Schmich, columnist for the *Chicago Tribune*

I don't see here on this side; but I will see on the other side. I know I'll get to see. I know I'll get to walk those golden streets and I'll get to see Shadrach, Meshach and Abednego; and I'll get to see the Lord. Oh yes I will.

—Ronnie Milsap, singer, during an interview
with the Christian Broadcasting Network

I know what I'm having 'em put on my tombstone: "I have nothing more to say."

—Ted Turner, entrepreneur

Now hoppin'-john was F. Jasmine's very favorite food. She had always warned them to wave a plate of rice and peas before her nose when she was in her coffin, to make certain there was no mistake; for if a breath of life was left in her, she would sit up and eat, but if she smelled the hoppin'-john, and did not stir, then they could just nail down the coffin and be certain she was truly dead.

—Carson McCullers, author, *The Member of the Wedding*

When my mother died, and when my father died, it's big. Our parents are giants; they're titans of our lives, so of course it's going to be a big deal.

—Loudon Wainwright III, humorist and author

When they look back on me I want 'em to remember me not for all my wives, although I've had a few, and certainly not for any mansions or high livin' money I made and spent. I want 'em to remember me simply for my music.

—Jerry Lee Lewis, singer

Death the last voyage, the longest, and the best.
—Thomas Wolfe, author

Now then, the funeral party. In case you all ain't noticed, the first three letters of the word funeral spell fun.

—Olive Ann Burns, author, *Cold Sassy Tree*

Death is no more than passing from one room into another. But there's a difference for me, you know. Because in that other room I shall be able to see.

—Helen Keller, author

I wrote that song in St Augustine, Florida. We went to a cookout on the beach and everybody forgot to bring their guitars. I was standing by the ocean and there was a breeze and the words kept coming to me. It's about all the rock stars I liked that died had come back and were playing a show just for me. Like Jimi Hendrix, Janis Joplin and Jim Morrison. And eventually more of course.

—Hughie Thomasson about the song,
"Green Grass and High Tides"

Separate we come,
and separate we go.
And this be it known,
Is all that we know.

—Conrad Aiken, poet

Time goes by so fast. Nothin' can
outrun it. Death commences too early—
almost before you're half-acquainted
with life—you meet the other.
—Tennessee Williams, *Cat on a Hot Tin Roof*

I miss all of my old friends who have passed away. Sometimes you just don't understand why they were taken so soon. I loved and miss Johnny Cash. I miss my old buddy Johnny Paycheck, who happens to be buried in an area of the cemetery that I bought for my family.

—George Jones, singer

Don't go to the grave with life unused.

—Bobby Bowden, former football coach
at Florida State University

Grief is like the wake behind a boat. It starts out as a huge wave that follows close behind you and is big enough to swamp and drown you if you suddenly stop moving forward. But if you do keep moving, the big wake will eventually dissipate. And after a long time, the waters of your life get calm again, and that is when the memories of those who have left begin to shine as bright and as enduring as the stars above.

—Jimmy Buffett, singer

The truth is, honey, I've enjoyed my life. I've had a hell of a good time.
—Ava Gardner, actress

I believe that all roads lead to the same place—and that is wherever all roads lead to.

—Willie Nelson, singer

I love this place. . . . I've got a spot already picked out where I want 'em to put me when I die—up there on that ole hill near the stadium. I want to be there so I can hear all them people cheering my Tigers on Saturdays . . . then I won't have to go Heaven; I'll already be there.

—Frank Howard,
former football coach at Clemson University

I would like to be remembered as a—somebody who could rock your soul or make you cry with a song. And somebody who's kind, who loved to laugh, and loved his God.

—Gregg Allman, musician

There was no noise, no tremble, just peace. Oh god. I realize as a woman how lucky I am. I was there when that wonderful creature drifted into my life and I was there when she drifted out. It was the most precious moment of my life.

—Sally Field as M'Lynn, *Steel Magnolias*

Be thankful for what you have; you'll end up having more. If you concentrate on what you don't have, you will never, ever have enough.

—Oprah Winfrey, entertainer

I tell young people—including my granddaughter—there is no shortcut in life. You have to take it one step at a time and work hard. And you have to give back.

—Hank Aaron, former outfielder for the Atlanta Braves

*Somewhere along the line we stopped
believing we could do anything. And if we
don't have our dreams, we have nothing.*
—Billy Bob Thornton, actor

My father used to say that it's never too late to do anything
you wanted to do. And he said, 'You never know what you
can accomplish until you try.

—Michael Jordan, former professional
basketball player for the Chicago Bulls

Be with someone who is kind. I think that's it. Just to love
one another was the thing I would want to do. It's a thing
that you can't stop doing.

—Garth Brooks, singer

Second place is just the first-place loser.

—Dale Earnhardt, professional race-car driver

Too many people spend money they haven't earned to buy
things they don't want to impress people they don't like.

—Will Rogers, humorist and actor

The best way to persuade people is with your ears—by
listening to them.

—Dean Rusk, fifty-fourth US secretary of state

If you're gonna sing, sing loud.
—Travis Tritt, singer

If you're looking for a dress to wear to an event, put it on with the heels that you're going to wear and walk around the room and make sure you feel comfortable in it.
—Vanna White, *Wheel of Fortune* letter turner

My mom raised my two sisters, my brother and me with this simple advice: "Let 'em know you're there." I've adapted that to "If you don't ask, you don't get."
—Katie Couric, journalist

You do what you can for as long as you can, and when you finally can't, you do the next best thing. You back up but you don't give up.
—Chuck Yeager, aviator

I always tell my kids if you lay down, people will step over you. But if you keep scrambling, if you keep going, someone will always, always give you a hand. Always. But you gotta keep dancing, you gotta keep your feet moving.
—Morgan Freeman, actor

If a friend asks a favor, you should grant it if it is reasonable; if not, tell him plainly why you cannot: You will wrong him and wrong yourself by equivocation of any kind.
—Gen. Robert E. Lee, commander of the Confederate Army

Sadly, some folks want others to feel their pain, to hurt as much as they do—or more. My grandmother once told me to avoid colds and angry people whenever I could. It's sound advice.
—Walter Inglis Anderson, artist and writer

Never insult an alligator until after you have crossed the river.
—Cordell Hull, former US secretary of state under Franklin D. Roosevelt

Honesty is the first chapter in the book of wisdom.
—Thomas Jefferson, third president of the United States

You've got to accentuate the positive,
Eliminate the negative,
Latch on to the affirmative,
Don't mess with Mister In-Between.
—Johnny Mercer, lyricist

Age is a case of mind over matter. If you don't mind it, it don't matter.

—Satchel Paige, former pitcher for the Cleveland Indians

As you walk down the fairway of life you must smell the roses, for you only get to play one round.

—Ben Hogan, late professional golfer

If you don't ever get out of your comfort zone you will never make it to the end zone.

—Deborah Roberts, journalist

If you live long enough, you'll make mistakes. But if you learn from them, you'll be a better person. It's how you handle adversity, not how it affects you. The main thing is never quit, never quit, never quit.

—Bill Clinton, forty-second president of the United States

Procrastination is the bad habit of putting off until the day after tomorrow what should have been done the day before yesterday.

—Napoleon Hill, writer

You better have an anchor in life. It doesn't matter if you're a Division I head football coach or Joe Schmo from Okemoh. Bad things happen. If you're not anchored, you're going to be washed away.
   —Dabo Swinney, football coach, Clemson University

Humor makes our heavy burdens light and smooths the rough spots in our pathways.
   —Sam Ervin, former US senator from North Carolina

Failure happens all the time. It happens every day in practice. What makes you better is how you react to it.
—Mia Hamm, professional soccer player

Your career is not going to go the way you planned. It is impossible at the age of twenty-three to pick the right industry, the right company, and you can visualize what you're going to be doing in your forties, fifties, and sixties, but chances are that it's going to be something quite different. So remain open to opportunities and change.
   —Sallie Krawcheck, businesswoman and author

The grass may look greener on the other side, but believe me, it's just as hard to cut.
                        —Little Richard Penniman, singer

If you see something that is not right, not fair, not just, you have a moral obligation to do something about it.

—John Lewis, activist and US congressman from Georgia

Don't ever criticize yourself. Don't go around all day long thinking, "I'm unattractive, I'm slow, I'm not as smart as my brother." God wasn't having a bad day when he made you . . . If you don't love yourself in the right way, you can't love your neighbor. You can't be as good as you are supposed to be.

—Joel Osteen, televangelist

Banish the words *I can't* from your vocabulary. Remember: If *can't* equals *won't*, *can* equals *will*.

—Phyllis George, journalist

Strive to be the very best you can be. Run the race against yourself and not the guy in the other lane. The reason I say that is, as long as you give it 110 percent, you are going to succeed. But as long as you're trying to beat the guy over there, you are worried about him; you're not worrying about how you've got to perform.

—Herschel Walker, former professional football player

Walking with a friend in the dark is better than walking alone in the light.

—Helen Keller, author

We must develop and maintain the capacity to forgive. He who is devoid of the power to forgive is devoid of the power to love. There is some good in the worst of us and some evil in the best of us. When we discover this, we are less prone to hate our enemies.

—Martin Luther King Jr., clergyman and activist

The river is constantly turning and bending and you never know where it's going to go and where you'll wind up. Following the bend in the river and staying on your own path means that you are on the right track. Don't let anyone deter you from that.

—Eartha Kitt, actress

Obstacles don't have to stop you. If you run into a wall, don't turn around and give up. Figure out how to climb it, go through it, or work around it.

—Michael Jordan, former basketball player for the Chicago Bulls

One hundred percent my mother, who would always say, "If you want something done, do it yourself." She must have said that a hundred times to me—as a child, as a young woman, yesterday on the phone.

—Reese Witherspoon, actress

You've got to continue to grow, or you're just like last night's cornbread—stale and dry.

—Loretta Lynn, singer-songwriter and author, *Loretta Lynn: Coal Miner's Daughter*

Always dream and shoot higher than you know you can do. Do not bother just to be better than your contemporaries or predecessors. Try to be better than yourself.

—William Faulkner, writer

Sometimes the best things are right in front of you; it just takes some time to see them.

—Gladys Knight, singer

No looking back. Life goes one way only, and whatever opinions you hold about the past have nothing to do with anything but your own damn weakness. Nothing changes what already happened. It will always have happened. You either let it break you down or you don't.

—Charles Frazier, writer

Find something that you're really interested in doing in your life. Pursue it, set goals, and commit yourself to excellence. Do the best you can.

–Chris Evert, retired professional tennis player

When you reach out to others in need, when you reach out to the world, you really do have a satisfying life by helping others.

–Laura Bush, former first lady of the United States

Put your trust in the Lord and go ahead. Worry gets you no place.

–Roy Acuff, singer

Associate yourself with men of good quality if you esteem your own reputation; for 'tis better to be alone than in bad company.
–George Washington, first president of the United States

You have to keep your goal in mind and never lose sight of it. I envisioned myself winning the heavyweight title for ten years before I actually captured it. If you're not driven to do your best, you'll never reach the level of excellence in your life.

–George Foreman, author, *God in My Corner: A Spiritual Memoir*

I was probably twenty-one or twenty-two years old when I realized the prose that I live by, which is, "You get what you give." The more good deeds that you could do in your life, the more fulfilling and enriched your life is going to be. I truly believe that.

—Zac Brown, singer

You never have to wait long, or look far, to be reminded of how thin the line is between being a hero or a goat.

—Mickey Mantle, former outfielder for the New York Yankees

These are the things I learned: share everything, play fair. Don't hit people. Put things back where you found them. Clean up your own mess. Don't take things that aren't yours. Say you're sorry when you hurt somebody. Wash your hands before you eat. Warm cookies and cold milk are good for you. Live a balanced life. Learn some and think some and draw some and paint and sing and dance and play and work some every day. Take a nap every afternoon, and, when you go out into the world, watch for traffic, hold hands, and stick together.

—Robert Fulghum, author, *All I Really Need to Know I Learned in Kindergarten*

Go out on a limb. That's where the fruit is.
—Jimmy Carter, thirty-ninth president of the United States

You'll never get mixed up if you simply tell the truth. Then you don't have to remember what you have said, and you never forget what you have said.

—Sam Rayburn, forty-third speaker of the US House of Representatives

Depend upon yourself. Make your judgment trustworthy by trusting it. You can develop good judgment as you do the muscles of your body—by judicious, daily exercise. To be known as a man of sound judgment will be much in your favor.

—Grantland Rice, sportswriter

I read once, which I loved so much, that this great physicist who won a Nobel Prize said that every day when he got home, his dad asked him not what he learned in school but his dad said, "Did you ask any great questions today?" And I always thought, What a beautiful way to educate kids—that we're excited by their questions, not by our answers and whether they can repeat our answers.

—Diane Sawyer, journalist

The game of life is a lot like football. You have to tackle your problems, block your fears, and score your points when you get the opportunity.

—Lewis Grizzard, author,
Gettin' It On: A Down Home Treasury

You possess a nonrenewable resource, which is headed toward total depletion, and that resource is time. You can either invest your life or let it dribble through your fingers like sand in an hourglass. If there is ever a time to redeem every second, every minute, it is now. You may never have tomorrow. You can't count your days, but with the Lord as your Savior, you can make your days count.

—Billy Graham, evangelist

The single biggest time waster in the world is not completing what you start.

—John Nance Garner, thirty-second US vice president

INDEX

Gardner, Ava, 14, 183
Garner, Jennifer, 84
Garner, John Nance, 126, 196
Gentry, Bobbie, 38
George, Phyllis, 190
Gibson, Althea, 99
Gibson, Thomas, 84
Gillespie, Dizzy, 86
Gill, Vince, 170
Glines, Abbi, 86
Glock, Allison, 13
Gowdy, Trey, 131
Graham, Billy, 118, 171, 196
Graham, Franklin, 131
Graham, Lindsey, 132
Graham, Patricia H., 7
Grant, Amy, 118
Greene, Amy, 45
Greene, Melissa Faye, 53
Griffith, Andy, 13
Grisham, John, 6, 34, 49, 119
Grizzard, Lewis, 52, 157, 171, 196

H

Hager, Jenna Bush, 151
Haley, Nikki, 100, 109
Hall, Carla, 51
Hamer, Fannie Lou, 111
Hamill, Pete, 139
Hamm, Mia, 189
Hammond, James Henry, 27
Han, Jenny, 50
Hanks, Tom, 148
Harvey, Steve, 78, 171
Hayes, Hunter, 88
Heart, Blake O'Hara, 173
Heaton, Tim, 25, 77, 146
Henry, O., 36, 164, 177
Henry, Patrick, 23

Hewitt, Jennifer Love, 12
Hiaasen, Carl, 38
Hill, Faith, 13, 50, 165
Hill, Napoleon, 188
Hobby, Oveta Culp, 178
Hogan, Ben, 188
Hogan, Hulk, 66
Holt, Kimberly Willis, 35
Holyfield, Evander, 110, 147
Howard, Frank, 70, 184
Howard, Ron, 77
Huckabee, Mike, 34, 110, 129
Hull, Cordell, 29, 187
Hunter, Clementine, 83
Hunter-Gault, Charlayne, 96
Hunter, Holly, 15, 160

J

Jackson, Alan, 14
Jackson, Andrew, 24
Jackson, Bo, 66
Jackson, Jesse, 9, 126
Jackson, Keith, 4, 70
Jackson, Shoeless Joe, 71
James, Harry, 52
James, Theo, 40
Jefferson, Thomas, 26, 187
Jindal, Bobby, 160
Johnson, James Weldon, 101
Johnson, Lyndon B., 95, 128, 164
Jones, Bobby, 63, 67
Jones, George, 183
Jones, James Earl, 54, 154
Jones, Tommy Lee, 82
Joplin, Janis, 17
Jordan, Michael, 96, 185, 191
Judd, Ashley, 18

ABOUT THE AUTHOR

Polly Powers Stramm is a veteran journalist who has written and/or co-authored ten books. She is also a longtime newspaper reporter whose column "Polly's People" appears in the *Savannah Morning News*. She is the author of *Bless Your Heart & Mind Your Mama: Sassy, Sweet and Silly Southernisms*.